BIATHLON
Training and Racing Techniques

KEN SOUZA
with Bob Babbitt

CONTEMPORARY
BOOKS

CHICAGO · NEW YORK

Library of Congress Cataloging-in-Publication Data

Souza, Ken.
       Biathlon : training and racing techniques / Ken Souza with
Bob Babbitt.
       p.   cm.
       Includes index.
       ISBN 0-8092-4369-5 : $8.95
       1. Running races.   2. Bicycle racing.   3. Running—
Training.   4. Cycling—Training.   I. Babbitt, Bob.   II. Title.
GV1061.S57   1989
796.93'2—dc20   89-31989
                                         CIP

To my friend David Bailey, formerly one of the best moto-cross racers in the world. One day you'll leave that wheelchair behind and soar again.

Copyright © 1989 by Bob Babbitt
All rights reserved
Published by Contemporary Books, Inc.
180 North Michigan Avenue, Chicago, Illinois 60601
Manufactured in the United States of America
International Standard Book Number: 0-8092-4369-5

Published simultaneously in Canada by Beaverbooks, Ltd.
195 Allstate Parkway, Valleywood Business Park
Markham, Ontario L3R 4T8 Canada

CONTENTS

Foreword   v
Acknowledgments   vii
Introduction   ix

1 A Short History of the Biathlon   1

2 Cycling   11

▶ ChekPoint: Self-Massage   30

▶ Indoor Turbo Training   33

3 Running   41

▶ ChekPoint: Stretching   55

4 Putting It All Together: A 12-Week Training
      Plan   63

▶ ChekPoint: Building Abdominal Strength   80

▶ Ken Souza's Year-Long Training Program   85

▶ Biathlon Survival Kit   87

5 Training Tips for the Hardcore Biathlete   89

▶ Chekpoint: Injuries   102

6 The Race   105

▶ ChekPoint: Using Sports Massage   122

▶ The Well-Dressed Biathlete   126

7 Alternative Training   127

▶ ChekPoint: The Biathlon Trouble Shooter's Guide   135

8 Biathlons Around the Country: The Biggest, the
     Best, and a Few of the Rest   139

▶ ChekPoint: Strengthening for the Biathlon   153

9 Biathletes Are People Too   155

10 Training Clubs to Get You Going   181

Appendix   187
Index   191

Frank Shorter, lean and mean at the Desert Princess World Biathlon Championships.

FOREWORD

Frank Shorter, the 1972 Olympic gold medalist in the marathon, had never done a biathlon when he entered his first one in February 1989. It was the Desert Princess World Biathlon Championships, held in Palm Springs, and it was one heckuva way for a rookie to start. The Desert Princess race directors, Greg Klein and Brenda Clark, had brought in top 40-to-45-year-old-olds from all over the country to give Shorter a little competition, but he showed everyone that a runner can easily adapt to riding competitively on a bicycle. Shorter, who lives in Boulder, Colorado, had to do a lot of his training during the winter months indoors. "I trained by riding intervals on the turbo trainer and then getting off and running hard on the treadmill," says Shorter. "I'd hit the treadmill at 5:30 per mile and make myself go hard even before starting my running intervals."

On a treadmill, a 5:30 pace is about equivalent to a 5:10 mile. Frank Shorter was learning to run quickly after finishing the bike ride, the key to being a good biathlete.

The Desert Princess World Biathlon Championships begins with a 10K run, followed by a 62K (40-mile) bike and finishing with another 10K run. The questions about

Shorter before the race were, one, could he ride the bike fast enough and, two, could he run after riding the bike? After a 32-minute first run, he had established a four-minute lead over former Olympic cyclist and 1981 Ironman winner John Howard. Shorter lost his lead when Howard passed him about 20 miles into the bike ride. "I knew that if he got 10 minutes on me I was dead," recalls Shorter. "If not, I knew I had a chance."

As he approached the finish of the 40-mile bike ride, Shorter knew that he was still in the hunt to catch Howard, the guy who was voted the best cyclist of the 1970s and who holds the world speed record on a bicycle at more than 150 miles per hour. "It felt really good when I came up the road on the bike and didn't see Howard," says Shorter. "Then I knew I had a chance."

Howard had a five-minute lead coming off the bike. All of Shorter's indoor bike-to-run training was about to pay major dividends. He made the transition from bike to run and immediately made up lost ground. "One guy told me I picked up one-and-a-half minutes in the first mile," said an ecstatic Shorter after the race. "My legs felt awkward until the first turn. Then they were fine."

Shorter knew that he was gaining, but was it going to be enough? "At the four-mile mark some guy told me that I was four minutes down," says Shorter. "Then I thought 'Hey, he might be one of John Howard's buddies,' "

Just past the five-mile mark, Shorter spotted Howard up ahead, barely moving. Shorter passed him and went on winning the biathlon world championship—and his first biathlon! Shorter's final 10K was 34:01 after a 1:45 bike and an opening 10K run of 32 minutes.

"I didn't suffer as much during the biathlon as I do during a marathon," Shorter says. "It was a lot more fun." Fun? Yeah, fun is the name of the biathlon game. Frank Shorter *guarantees* you'll enjoy yourself. And you can trust the guy. Remember, he became the masters biathlon world champion on his first try. What are *you* waiting for? Lace up those running shoes, hop on that bike, and get going. You'll love it!

ACKNOWLEDGMENTS

Even though the sports of running, cycling, biathlon, and triathlon are thought to be individual sports, the reality is that no one goes it alone. When I first moved to San Diego to train for triathlon, I wanted to improve as a swimmer, cyclist, and runner. I knew that the best way to do that was to surround myself with the best people around, the guys who were winning all of the races. Those guys were Scott Molina, Scott Tinley, and Mark Allen. They were my heroes, but they didn't seem to mind my asking questions and tagging along on bike rides and runs. Of course, it didn't hurt my credibility when I kicked their butts during a few workouts along the way.

What I'm trying to say is that you don't get good at anything by just going out and doing it all by yourself. You need people to ride and run with, people to support you when you're down, and people to get you back on track when your head starts to swell a bit. If there's one thing I would like you to gain from this book, it is realizing the importance of using the human resources around you.

Anytime you train, it's always more enjoyable to work with a group. I want to take this opportunity to thank my group: Molina, Tinley, and Allen, of course, plus my agent, Murphy Reinschreiber. Lois Schwartz, Bob Babbitt, Ken McAlpine, Gary Hooker, Dan Rock, Bob Macy, and massage therapist Paul Chek were all instrumental in making this book a reality.

And to you readers: Enjoy the book. More importantly, enjoy your training. See you on the road!

Kenny Souza

INTRODUCTION

In my first triathlon, way back in 1984 in Phoenix, I finished about 300th out of the water. (It wasn't hard to find my bike in the rack; it was the only one there!) Believe it or not, I eventually finished in the top 25. You know when you drive on the highway and bugs come rushing at you and sacrifice themselves on your windshield? That's the way those other competitors looked to me on the bike-and-run course. The truth was unmistakable. As a triathlete, I made one heck of a *bi*athlete.

But at that time the only sport in town was the triathlon. And since I knew that my swim-like-a-Redwood style wouldn't do me much good in the short distance (1,500-meter swim/ 25-mile bike/ 6.2-mile run) world of triathlons, I began training for the longer events so I could make up for lost time by hammering my brains out in the bike and the run.

I put this book together to get you ready for a 5K run/30K bike/5K run biathlon. If you compare the training program I've set up for you to the one I do myself, you're bound to wonder, why the discrepancy in mileage?

It's very simple. I got into the habit of megamileage because I knew how hard I would have to work to make up ground on the likes of Scott Molina, Mark Allen, Mike Pigg, and Scott Tinley in a long-distance triathlon such as Nice or the Ironman. To make up 10–15 minutes on the best in the world, I had to put in some outrageous mileage. Five-hundred-mile weeks on the bike were not uncommon for me. And because that is what I am used to, it's hard for me to break away from long-distance training. But I don't recommend workouts that stress a lot of mileage when you're just starting out, so I've also provided some workouts for you, the budding biathlete.

Fortunately, the sport of biathlon has caught on in a big way, and all the other nonswimmers of the world can unite around shorter workouts and higher intensity. According to the Coors Light people who put on the highly acclaimed 12-city Coors Light Biathlon Series during the summer and fall of 1988, nearly 50 percent of the entrants had never entered a multisport event before. That tells me that there are a lot of runners and cyclists out there who hate swimming and totally ignored the triathlon movement. Since the series was extremely successful, it also leads me to believe that maybe there are a lot of working runners and cyclists with families who just could not find the time to learn two new sports. Well, if you're only a runner or cyclist, you'll have to pick up just one new sport. And if you're a complete rookie, learning two sports is sure a heckuva lot easier than learning three.

The purpose of this book is to combine your "hobbies" under a very enjoyable umbrella called the biathlon. For the working person with limited training time, biathlon is your ticket to fun and frolic. Even if you are beginning with absolutely no background in riding or running, know that in three months you will be ready for your first run-bike-run event. My plan isn't to make you into just a biathlete, but to transform you into a fast, competitive biathlete. You have my word on it.

1
THE SHORT HISTORY OF THE BIATHLON

Because of the rapid growth of the triathlon, there was no real biathlon movement to speak of until the mid-1980s. Dan Honig, founder of the Big Apple Biathlon Club in New York, put on his first run-bike-run event in New York in 1984. It drew 500 participants. That first-ever official event, the Brooklyn Biathlon, consisted of a three-mile run, a 16-mile ride, and another three-mile run. In 1989, Honig will put on eight events throughout the boroughs of New York City, averaging around 650 participants per event.

Honig's success with the biathlon is just a sample of the popularity and growth of the sport. In four short years, the number of biathlon events across the country has grown from 18 to more than 500. Recently, a surge of biathlon events has occurred nationwide, thanks to the interest of major corporations such as the Coors Brewing Company, which sponsors a 12-city race series from August to November. According to the *New York Times,* the biathlon is no longer the triathlon's poor sister. More than 300,000 athletes competed in 500 running-cycling events this year, compared to a few thousand that participated in 15 such events in 1984.

According to top triathlete Scott Molina, the biathlons he recalls from the early and late 1970s were all swim-run events. One of the first biathlons, in 1974, was the Tug's Tavern swim-run-swim, initiated by 1979 Ironman winner Tom Warren of Pacific Beach, California. Warren was one of the pioneers of the triathlon as well as the biathlon.

Throughout the 1970s there were numerous short swim-run-swim biathlons and triathlons held around San Diego's Mission Bay. The people involved in the run-swim-run events and the early triathletes were runners looking for diversion. Triathletes and biathletes were, by and large, the type of hyperactive kids who couldn't sit still in class. Running alone just wasn't enough. They were bored. Biathlons and triathlons gave them an outlet. Tired of running? Ride the bike. Fed up with cycling? How about a quarter-mile swim in the ocean? The cycling "in" crowd thought the idea of combining sports was frivolous and basically ignored the movement. But for burned-out runners, it was a chance to branch out, to experiment with another discipline.

WHO DOES THE BIATHLON?

According to Honig, 75 percent of the people who enter his events (eight biathlons and four triathlons) come from a running background; only 5 percent come from a swimming background.

For busy people without a lot of time on their hands, the biathlon makes a lot of sense. For example, at the base of the biathlon is the runner. The runner tends to be an individual in the middle-to-upper-income bracket who is college educated and has a demanding job and family. This person does not have the time, or the desire to pick up two sports, to learn how to swim *and* ride the bike to compete in triathlons. The runner can adapt to cycling a lot more easily than to swimming. And the workouts in both run-

Photo by Lois Schwartz

This is a photo from one of my first-ever biathlon events back in 1985.

ning and cycling can be very social. There is nothing more enjoyable than a casual 50-miler in the country with a few friends. If the pace is not too intense, chatting about the family and the office can be downright therapeutic. I know that more than one business deal has been consummated on the bike. I've heard of athletes negotiating appearance fees with race directors during these casual group get-togethers.

Cycling also gives you range, something that running doesn't. In an hour you can ride 20–25 miles from your house. Unless you are one great runner, 10–11 miles is probably the maximum distance you can go in that time. Cycling is a lot easier on the joints of the body and can truly supplement your running workouts.

Runners tend to adapt to the biathlon very quickly. This is 2:35 marathoner Laurie Clare, of San Diego, in her first-ever event, the 1988 Bud Light Ontario National Championships. She led the race after the five-mile run but dropped back to fifth during the 20-mile ride that followed.

Photo by Lois Schwartz

THE GROWTH OF THE BIATHLON

The increase in biathlon participation over the past few years can be attributed to a number of factors, other than that the biathlon is just good, clean fun:

1. **Better focus.** Triathletes are often looking for ways to refine their skills. Without the swim, the triathlete can focus on just two skills for the duration of the biathlon season. It's also nice for the triathlete to get the water out of his ears and the goggle marks off of his face once in a while.

2. **Readiness**. The Coors Light Biathlon Series survey during the summer of 1988 showed that nearly 50 percent of the entrants in the 12-city race series had never entered a multisport event before. This means a lot of runners totally ignored the triathlon movement of the early and mid-1980s and are only now ready to get involved.

3. **Time**. Without swimming, training time can be more easily balanced with a job and family. The biathlete-come-lately can schedule both base-building and speed-building work in two sports without turning off the family or the boss.

4. **The I-hate-this-because-I'm-lousy-at-it syndrome**. Runners are by definition lean and mean. They also, for the most part, float like a rock. No one wants to go to swim workout and consistently be the worst swimmer in the pool. When you have limited time, you want to feel successful.

5. **Weather**. For a majority of the country, triathlon is a warm-weather sport. This means that on the East Coast and in the Midwest, triathlons have to be held when the air and the water are warm—at the most, three months a year. Of course, wet suits make the cold water a little less of a factor, but triathlons are still limited to the summer months. Because no swimming is involved, biathlons can be held pretty much all year long. Using mountain bikes, tights, and gloves, a 5Krun/40K bike/5K run event can be held even in the middle of winter.

BIATHLONS AND LOCALITY

New York's Dan Honig feels you can put on a biathlon virtually anywhere. "If we have three months of beach weather here a year," says Honig, "the last thing a local municipality wants to do is schedule a triathlon that will monopolize that beach. They guard their beaches like gold. You want to put on an event on Long Island? Forget it! But it's no problem to get a permit 20 miles from Long Island for a biathlon."

Honig also feels that a biathlon is a better business investment for the race director. Adding a swim does not increase your work load just 33 percent; it increases it 100 percent. "I can put on two biathlons in the time it takes me to prepare for one triathlon," says Honig. "It's just that much easier. The fact that you have a swim in your race makes the other events that much harder to put on. You have to adapt the bike and run to the swim. Give me a road, and I'll give you a biathlon. No sweat. Give me a beach, and now I've got to get to the road that is a quarter mile from the water. I've got to deal with sand, swim caps, lifeguards, surfboards, wave swim starts, and cold water. I've got to take over the beach for two hours. There need to be changing areas so people can get out of their swimsuits and into their cycling outfits. You just don't need a changing area at a biathlon."

Even with weather limitations, Honig puts on races from February through November. In the winter he puts on his Fat-Tire Biathlon Series, with one event in February and one in March. The distances are 2 miles, 10 miles, and 2 miles. I can't imagine what it would be like to compete in February, but at least Honig is offering the die-hard biathletes the opportunity to compete year-round.

Joe Krotovil, race director of the Princeton Biathlon, found that his sponsors really enjoyed their involvement with his biathlon. "They were able to sit up over the street and watch the racers go by," he says. "Our course is looped through the city, which is something I couldn't do if I had to be near the water." The biathlon concept gives Krotovil the opportunity to bring his event smack downtown and positively influence the athletes as well as the sponsors and spectators. "With a looped course," says Krotovil, "I can offer primes for the leader at the end of each bike and run lap. This gets the spectators *and* the athletes into the event." And it doesn't hurt any to have your sponsor sitting upstairs watching athletes and spectators going into a frenzy at the event *they* sponsor. "After the race in 1988," he continues, "my sponsors told me to sign them up for next year."

Joe Krotovil dabbles in both biathlons and triathlons, but he can see the writing on the wall. "I think the biathlon has

Photo by Lois Schwartz

Two of the biggest names in triathlon like to use the biathlon as a way to stay fit during their off-season. On the left is five-time Nice Triathlon champion Mark Allen, and on the right is two-time Ironman champion Scott Tinley.

the potential to get bigger than triathlon," he says. "You can hold a biathlon anywhere under any weather conditions. I'm personally investing more in the biathlon market than triathlon."

The race-directing team of Greg Klein and Brenda Clark originally wanted to put on a triathlon. But when you live in Palm Springs, you have to go with what you've got. What Klein and Clark had was a willing sponsor in the Desert Princess resort and condominium complex. But how

Everyone and anyone can ride a bike. Therefore, everyone and anyone can do a biathlon.

Photo by Lois Schwartz

could they attract athletes out to the desert in the middle of winter, the triathlon off-season, to compete in a brand-new event?

Showing great presence of mind, Klein and Clark signed Scott Molina to enter the first race back in November 1986. Signing Molina gave the event credibility and helped draw a big crowd to Palm Springs for their first 10 K run/62 K bike/10 K run event. When Molina was beaten by unknown professional triathlete Brad Kearns of Los Angeles, the multisport world sat up and took notice. "Ninety percent of the people, including me, picked Molina to win," says Klein.

There was something appealing about an event that took about the same amount of time as a marathon. At the first race, most of the top athletes had a very fast first 10K and followed that with great cycling times. It was that final 10K, on the same course as the first, that put the name Desert Princess right up there with some of the nation's hardest events. I dropped out during that first race, and I was one of the prerace favorites. Bill Fulton, a good friend and Los Angeles triathlon series race director, told Greg Klein that I would dominate Klein's event. All I dominated was the DNF (did not finish) list. Kearns won again in the second race. This time I finished . . . but my second 10K was 47 minutes! Was I gaining a little bit of respect for that last 10K, what top biathlete Joel Thompson nicknamed "the dirt road from hell"? You bet I was. I remember talking with Scott Molina after that second race. He was having his problems too. Why was this run-bike-run stuff so hard? He reminded me that way back in 1983, when the Kauai Triathlon used to consist of a 1.2-mile swim, a 12-mile run, and a 56-mile bike ride, he couldn't run for nine full days afterward, even though he won the race. "I looked back at my training log," he told me. "Every day it said something like 'Can't run . . . too sore' or 'I can't believe it. . . . My legs still feel like lead.' "

Molina's problems were caused by the run-to-bike transition. Triathletes were used to bike-to-run, not run-to-bike. The bike takes a lot out of the legs, and the triathlete had to muscle through the run, losing a little speed in the process. But run-to-bike is different. You're able to run full out, as fast if not faster than regular race pace. Then you have to mount up and ride. Calf cramps at that first Desert Princess race bordered on an epidemic.

I finally won the third event of the first year, beating Kearns in February 1987. The rumblings were that even though I had won a number of shorter biathlons in New York, Colorado, and Arizona, I couldn't win a long race like the Desert Princess. I finally proved that I could.

I've found that the main difference between racing biathlons and triathlons is speed. For the pros, an event like the Desert Princess starts off with a 30–31 minute 10K. There's no chance to ease into a pace in a biathlon. I remember top biathlete George Pierce talking about racing the Princeton, New Jersey, biathlon during the summer of 1988. "I ran around 14:50 for the first 5K," he recalled, "and everyone was gone when I got to the transition area." It's true. Joel Thompson, Jeff Devlin, and I all ran in the 14:35 range.

My feeling is that when Mark Allen, Mike Pigg, Scott Tinley, and all the other top triathletes decided to do the Desert Princess events in the winter of 1988, they saw the previous 10K times and knew they'd have to run fast right from the gun. That training transferred over to their triathlons, and the run times during the summer of 1988 were a bit faster than before. At the USTS National Championships in Hilton Head, Mark Allen came in second to Mike Pigg after being three minutes down after the bike leg. Allen ran an outstanding 31:03 10K after the 1,500-yard swim and 40K bike ride.

FUTURE GROWTH

How big will biathlon become? It's hard to tell. The Desert Princess event features two races: the 10K run-62K bike-10K run and a 1.75-mile run/9-mile ride/1.75-mile run. The serious veterans specialize in the big one, while the rookies break into the circuit in the short race. At the first event of the 1988–1989 season, a seven-year-old completed the short event. Coors Light is talking about 15–20 cities for the 5K–40K–5K series in the next few years, and Dan Honig is putting on biathlons year-round. The sport is growing by leaps and bounds. More races, more athletes, more press, more prize money, more sponsorship. Buckle up those helmet straps, biathlon fans. We're in for one heckuva ride.

2
CYCLING

Prior to biathlons I started cycling because I was looking for something different. At the time, I was running track and cross-country for Wilson High School in Hacienda Heights, California, and biking seemed to me to be a nice, relaxing alternative. I'd spin around town on my Nishiki ten-speed, just enjoying myself and taking in the scenery.

From the beginning, cycling seemed to come naturally to me. But a lot of runners have trouble with cycling because they're so small and thin as a wisp that they often don't have the power needed to be a good cyclist. I was hardly Arnold Schwarzenegger, but I did seem to have a natural aptitude for the sport. I can remember people telling me, "Gee, you're strong" or "Wow, you sure ride fast," and that early feedback did a lot to keep me going. In fact, I may have moved along a bit too fast. I remember an early ride, not long after the 1984 Summer Olympics in Los Angeles, when I hooked up with some members of the Raleigh racing team. We were on a group ride when I suddenly found myself in the middle of a fast breakaway that included

Olympic gold medalist Steve Hegg. Here I was, this young nobody in a pink jersey and blue shorts, trying to hold my own alongside some of cycling's best. Heady stuff. So heady that I forgot to use my head. I strayed an inch or two off line, clipped someone's back wheel, and went down at 35 miles per hour. A painful reminder that I still had a lot to learn.

Cycling is a fun and fascinating sport—simple enough that anybody can do it, yet filled with so many intricacies that you'll always find yourself learning something new. There's no sense, though, in making unnecessary (or painful) mistakes yourself when you can learn from the unnecessary and painful mistakes of others.

BUYING THE RIGHT BIKE

The first step is buying a bike. But I already have a bike, you say. That may be true, but before you swear off the idea of a *new* bike, take a close look at old faithful. Chances are it's been sitting in the garage for a couple of years now, accumulating rust ever since you wheeled it off the Sears showroom floor. Cyclists are fond of saying that it isn't the bike but the rider that makes the machine go, but they're usually spouting this little gem of wisdom while seated on a $2,000 handcrafted European job. A good bike will make riding safer, easier, and far more pleasant. It's an essential investment.

How much does a good bike cost? That depends. Bikes, like riders, come in all shapes and sizes, and prices run the gamut, from as little as $150 all the way up to $3,000. If you are just getting started, plan on spending between $400 and $500 for a racing bike. For that price you'll get a bike that has all the features of a top-of-the-line machine, except it will be a bit heavier and have Japanese components rather than the pricier Italian parts. This really makes little difference; for most purposes the $500 bike is almost as good as the bike priced at $1,000 or more.

You might be tempted to go a bit lower, especially after

Photos courtesy of Giro

Your number one priority as a biathlete is to stay healthy and safe. Remember to *always* wear a bike helmet. Giro makes two types of lightweight helmets: the Aerohead, a great racing helmet (top), and the Prolight bicycling helmet (bottom).

you factor in the additional cost of cycling accessories like helmet, shorts, gloves, water bottles, and cleats. Don't. Bike quality falls drastically once you drop below $400. There's also another important consideration. After riding for a while, many cyclists decide to upgrade parts, adding a more expensive gear cluster, buying racing wheels, replacing handlebars. It's simply not worth fine-tuning a $200 bike; some of the parts you'll be adding may be worth almost as much as the bike. A bike in the $400-to-$500 price range will be more than sufficient for your immediate needs, giving you a capable machine to race and train on for at least several years. After that, you might want to consider upgrading.

Photo courtesy of Oakley

It's important to wear a pair of sunglasses while you ride or run in order to protect your eyes from the sun and the elements. The worst thing in the world is to be out riding your bike with no shades on a windy day. An eyeful of dirt is definitely no fun.

Deciding where to buy your bike is almost as important as choosing the bike. If you don't shop at a reputable bike store, you may find yourself walking out with a hole in your wallet and a bike you don't need. Find a store where the salespeople know their product—not fast-track, used-car-folks but bike racers and multisport athletes. Not only do these people understand bikes, but they also understand your needs. Choosing the right bike is not a simple matter, and a qualified, concerned salesperson makes all the difference.

If you choose the right shop, when you do go in to buy a bike *they'll* ask all the questions. Don't be too concerned that you don't know a thing about the latest technology. You don't have to be an expert to figure out whether or not a bike is right for you . . . there are only a few things you need to remember. First, test ride the bike. Sounds like basic common sense, but a surprising number of people hop on their bike for the first time *after* they get it home. You wouldn't buy a car without taking a spin around the block, would you? Purchasing a bike is no different.

It's also extremely important that your bike is a proper fit. Fitting a bike to the rider can be complicated and time

Now, you don't need to buy every new cycling gimmick that comes along. But you also don't want to let the cycling world leave you in the dust because you're riding outdated equipment. This is top cyclist John Howard on his turn-of-the-century two-wheeler. A lot of part-time biathletes feel that they don't train or race enough to "deserve" the newest and best equipment around. Wrong. If the pros have it and it makes you go faster . . . go for it!

consuming. It's a real science, beginning with the proper frame size and going all the way down to such minute details as handlebar size and seat positioning. In some cases fractions of an inch can make the difference between a comfortable and efficient ride, and strain and possible injuries. Dan Rock, a top-ranked amateur biathlete and owner of Moonlight Bikes in Encinitas, California, believes that there are thousands of cyclists out there who could be riding much more efficiently with just a few minor adjustments. Rock recommends you have the bike fitted when you buy it; have the shop mechanic fit you to your purchase before you even walk out the door. This serves two purposes. First, the work is done by a qualified professional, ensuring that you get the exact fit that's right for you. Second, it's a matter of sound economics. If you find you need a shorter handlebar stem or longer pedal crank arms, you can upgrade right then and simply be charged the difference. If you walk out of the store and then come back

Photo courtesy of Vortechs Design Group

The benefit of a clipless pedal is that it allows you to get in and out of it quickly and safely. Old-style pedals came equipped with a toe strap that went over the foot, which was both uncomfortable and difficult to get out of. The clipless systems, like the Vortechs Pedal (above), are now standard equipment on many bicycles.

Photo by Lois Schwartz

Bill Leach (leading) is one of the top masters triathletes and biathletes in the country. His aerodynamic handlebars help him to keep his elbows in, so his body is like an arrow cutting through the air. Besides making the rider more aerodynamic, these handlebars also are more comfortable because they help take weight off the arms and the shoulders and stress off the neck muscles.

The devices on the end of my handlebars are called *grip shifts*. This is a convenient place to have your shifters so you don't have to reach down to change gears and so you can stay aerodynamic the whole time.

Photo by Lois Schwartz

later, you'll have to buy the new piece outright, and you'll be stuck with the old (and useless) one to boot.

Rock also points out that many first-time buyers don't factor in the cost of cycling accessories, which can mount up and often come as a rude surprise. In my mind, every rider should have a helmet, bike computer, gloves, cycling shorts and a jersey, a water bottle and cage, cycling cleats, spare tires, a patch kit, and a pump. All of this will cost extra, something you have to consider. If the bike you are buying doesn't have clip-on pedals, I recommend getting them. Though they were designed with top-notch racers in mind, I think clip-on pedals are ideal for beginners; you're not strapped in, and you can click right out of them just like a ski binding. This can come in quite handy when you're forced to make a sudden stop.

A lot of biathletes now are using Scott or AERO 1 handlebars. Aerodynamically designed to minimize wind resistance, these bars position you so you're almost lying flat on the bike. These handlebars are all I use, and there's no doubt they work; they've revolutionized time-trial cycling, and they've helped me shave time off my races. However, they're not for the beginner, nor are they an easy transition. They make the bike more difficult to handle and, because of the aerodynamic position of your body, tend to stress different muscles, especially the hamstrings. If you don't accustom yourself to them gradually, you can really hurt yourself. If you're just getting started, hold off on this piece of technology. Getting used to riding a finely tuned racing bike can be challenging enough. Aerodynamic bars are something to consider later, when you decide to get a little more serious.

DEVELOPING CYCLING TECHNIQUE

Once properly equipped, you're ready to go, although my first words of advice are slow, slow, slow. Cycling, unlike running, is by nature a forgiving sport: it's easy on your muscles, and almost anyone can go out and keep up a decent pace. To make matters worse, odds are you'll be raring to go. You've got this new bike, and you're going to push yourself and your bike to the limit. You can't wait to tear up those roads.

For the first two weeks, however, I don't recommend going out the door at all. It may seem a bit unconventional, but I think it's important in the beginning to spend some time spinning on a turbo trainer. It's another investment, but I think it's well worth it. Good pedaling technique is the heart of cycling. Riding on a turbo trainer will teach you how to ride properly, and without distractions like hills and cars you'll really learn to turn the pedal cranks efficiently. It might be a bit boring, but the habits you pick up here will stand you in good stead. On a turbo trainer you can concentrate not just on the downstroke but also on practicing pulling back on the upstroke to insure getting the most out of each revolution. This isn't an easy technique

Photo by Bob Babbitt

Riding on a tandem with a friend is a good way to train. This way you can ride hard intervals together, head home, and then hop off and run.

to master, and two weeks on the turbo trainer won't do it; but it's a good start. Even if you live in southern California, a turbo trainer will definitely come in handy during the winter months.

When you first begin riding, it's a sort of feeling-out process. Your body is being introduced to an entirely new sport. New muscles are coming to life. You are getting a feel for your own fitness and capabilities. You should ride slowly and in an easy gear. One of the most common mistakes novice cyclists make is riding in too hard a gear; they grind along, legs pushing at the pedals as if mired in molasses. Not only is this inefficient, but it's also downright dangerous. There's no surer way of injuring yourself than putting unnecessary strain on unfit muscles. I don't care if you hold the state record in the mile run or captained the basketball team all four years in college. Cycling uses different muscles. Go easy. Enjoy the scenery. If you're reasonably fit, try a 15–20 miler. See how you feel. If you're sore the next day, your body is telling you to ease off. If you're fit as a fiddle, up the distance. Just use common sense.

If you're just getting started, I recommend you ride every other day, taking days off whenever you feel like it. As you start to feel stronger, ride two days in a row and then take a

Emilio Desoto (right) works hard to try to outclimb Joel Thompson (left) at the West Coast Biathlon Series in Los Angeles. Notice that when you climb hills using the aerodynamic handlebars, you need to change your hand position on the bars.

Photo by Lois Schwartz

day off. Keep the mileage down. Disregard intensity altogether.

Even now I don't often ride that fast, except when I'm in a
group ride and other riders are dictating the pace. Friends
who ride with me always seem surprised. "Gee," they'll say,
"you don't ride hard at all." In a sense, it's true. For a long
time I didn't do much speed work at all; only in the last two
years have I experimented with intervals. From the beginning, I simply chose a different type of suffering to condi-
tion me for the lung-searing speeds that are a part of today's
races.

A bicycle shoe for
the biathlete (like the
Avia shown) should
have a velcro strap
for quick in and out
plus a rigid sole for
stability and power.

Photo courtesy of Avia

I'm talking about hills and mountains. I've always loved
the mountains, and biking has given me the opportunity to
discover some beauties. I've spent months training in
Boulder, Colorado, charging up and down mountains you
wouldn't believe. But you don't need the Rockies to benefit
from what I believe to be one of the best conditioning tools.
Any hill will do.

When I first started riding, I made a habit of charging
each and every hill during my rides. When a hill loomed
ahead, I'd drop into a comfortable gear and storm up. It's an
old habit I've never dropped, and it's one of the major
reasons for my success. Hill climbing builds tremendous

Photo by Lois Schwartz

On a technical bike course, always remember to keep your head up and be prepared to lean into every turn.

strength. It also teaches you how to pedal correctly. Your cadence slows, and if you concentrate (and sometimes even if you don't!), you can feel the whole pedal stroke pushing down and pulling up. It's an invaluable tool for improving your technique and a great conditioner.

One of the most important skills you need to learn is how to ride in a straight line or, in cycling parlance, hold a line. Nothing infuriates (and scares) experienced cyclists more than a rider wobbling all over the road; you are a danger to yourself and worse yet (at least in the minds of the other cyclists) a danger to others. I learned this firsthand during my glorious Team Raleigh breakaway, and it's a lesson I wouldn't want anyone to experience if he or she can avoid it. Fortunately, learning to hold a line is a straightforward exercise: find a lightly traveled road and ride with your front wheel glued to the white line along the shoulder. With

Photo by Sandra Small

So you want to get used to riding in a pack? Maybe you should try one of the many group rides that have become so popular. This photo is of the Rosarito-Ensenada Fun Ride in Mexico, which is held in the fall and spring each year. And just how many riders are there in this group? Try 16,000!

practice, holding a line will become habit. You'll no longer be a menace, and you'll also be a much more effective cyclist—the shortest distance between two points will always be a straight line.

Learning what gear to ride in is also crucial. If you want to ride fast, you have to learn to ride efficiently, getting as much power as you can without grinding yourself to a pulp. As I mentioned before, many novice cyclists ride in far too difficult a gear; if you are laboring, you are probably in too hard a gear. Some cyclists go to the other extreme, spinning the pedals like a gerbil on a treadmill. This is a pointless exercise that gets you nowhere fast; if you don't use some power on the pedals you might as well be standing still. You don't want pedaling to feel too easy. There's a happy medium here, and with time and experience you'll find it.

One other item bears mentioning. Many first-time cyclists simply can't seem to relax on the bike. Granted, this is

In bike-racing it is OK to draft, or stay right behind another cyclist. The rider in the back is doing a lot less work than the leader, who is breaking the wind. In a biathlon, however, you have to do all the work yourself because drafting is illegal.

difficult—you're hunched over on a seat that's rock hard and looks as if it's three sizes too small. Getting comfortable on the bike is a matter of conditioning and experience; with time you simply become more relaxed. But even experience is no guarantee you'll escape the soreness that seems to be your constant partner in the early going. I can stop riding for as little as a week, and when I get back on, sure enough, my butt hurts and my neck aches. Not to worry though. It will pass with time.

Pan American Gold Medalist John Howard brings up another good point. He recommends you concentrate on your breathing while you are riding, breathing smoothly and rhythmically and concentrating on the out breath. Stop reading for a second while you breathe in. Now exhale slowly. Relaxing, isn't it? Same premise on the bike. Unfortunately, in the excitement of it all, novice cyclists sometimes forget to breathe, inadvertently holding their breath and tightening up in the process. Of course, if you're riding hard, breathing smoothly and easily is out of the question. But during most of your riding it's easy to do. Again, just one more trick that comes with experience.

CYCLING FOR SPEED

I don't recommend doing speed work for at least two months. First build a base; then you can start attacking your cycling. Even then it's important to exercise caution. Speed work of any kind exponentially increases the risk of injury. Make sure your muscles are accustomed to the exercise *before* you start incorporating speed work into your training.

Speed work of some kind is essential if you want to be successful in the biathlon. Face it: for most of us the longest race we'll enter will be the standard 5-K run/30-K bike/5-K run. There are a few longer races (the 10K–60K–10K Desert Princess race, for example); most biathlons, though, are really sprints, and you should train for them as such. Why ride any farther than 40 miles if your longest ride is going to be only half that? You don't need to put in hundreds of miles to excel in the biathlon; there are plenty of examples of biathletes who do exceptionally well on what seems like ridiculously little training.

Speed work can take any number of forms. I choose to take on hills because I enjoy it, and that's what works for me. But you can really do whatever you want—your only limit is your own creativity. You can charge hills. You can set your watch or bike computer and ride hard for a minute then back off, recover, and do it again. You can let distance be your measure, riding hard for a half mile, then easing off, then riding hard for a half mile again. You can do any number of intervals you choose and pick any time or distance—10 one-minute sprints, seven half-mile sprints, four charges up a neighborhood hill with each followed by a coast back down. Maybe even a 10-mile time trial. The important things to remember are to warm up before you

Photo by Lois Schwartz

Scott Molina shows off his downhill technique. Notice how aerodynamic he gets.

hit it hard and ease into your interval workouts gradually. Don't do three-minute intervals the first time out. Start with 30 seconds, and work your way up.

How much speed work should you do? Three-time Olympic cyclist John Howard, who now lends his expertise to a number of top biathletes, recommends at least two speed sessions a week during the season. This is precisely what I do, riding hard during one training ride and using the weekend race as my second speed workout. During the off-season I take things a bit easier, alternating long rides with easy rides; my hard efforts are part of the long rides.

DEVELOPING POWER

In my opinion, a successful biathlete is equal parts speed and power. I've developed a lot of my power from going head-to-head with hills, but I'm also a firm believer in weight training. I started lifting in high school, and though I'm not always as disciplined as I'd like to be, I've been lifting fairly regularly since. Not everyone believes that weights are necessary. I've heard the argument again and again that the best thing for cycling is cycling. This may be a valid argument, but all I know is weights work for me. Some cyclists dread the thought of adding bulk, arguing that it's just something more to carry. They incorporate power into their training by doing intervals in big gears. As biathletes, though, our requirements are a bit different from cyclists, and I think weights serve a valuable purpose. My training, especially during the off-season, includes a fairly intensive weight-lifting program—everything from upper-body work to squats. I lift light weights with a lot of repetitions, and because I feel stronger, I race stronger. Weights are a matter of personal preference, but don't discount them just because others tell you to.

RIDING WITH A GROUP

Probably my hardest ride during the off-season is the Wednesday group ride. When I train in San Diego that ride borders on insanity. There's something about riding in a pack that gets people's competitive juices flowing; when you're riding with people like Mark Allen, Scott Tinley, and Scott Molina this borders on something comparable to bloodletting. I tend to be a bit lazy, and riding with others forces me to push myself harder than I might if I were riding alone. It's good to train alone, but I make it a habit to ride with a group at least once a week. Besides providing conditioning, riding with a pack can also be an invaluable learning tool. Most of the time the pack includes cyclists who are more experienced and can pass on all kinds of valuable advice, from how to tackle downhills to how to ride a pace line. These days most towns have bike clubs, triathlon clubs, or even biathlon clubs. The best way to find out whether your town offers a group ride is to go down to the local bike shop and ask. Odds are they'll say yes, and you're off to the races!

However, if you're just getting started on the bike I don't

recommend riding with a group right away. Riding shoulder-to-shoulder and wheel-to-wheel at 30 miles an hour can be an intimidating experience—even now I still get a little shaky at times. If you're a beginner, ride with a few friends or ride alone, but give yourself a little time to develop the bike-handling skills to survive in the pack.

My final word of advice is to relax. Don't forget what brought you out in the first place—fun. Even though I earn my living by training and racing, I wouldn't do it if I didn't like it. Sometimes on my long Saturday rides I'll ride off in no particular direction with no goal but to enjoy the ride. Some of these aimless meanderings have turned into real adventures—riding along fire trails through mountain passes with no idea where I'm headed. I'll get home eight hours and 120 miles later with nothing but sweat on my brow and a big smile on my face.

That's what it's all about.

Photo by Lois Schwartz

This rider says that he always gets dropped when he goes out cycling with his buddies, who call him "Pokey."

CHEKPOINT: SELF-MASSAGE by Paul Chek

Paul Chek is a massage therapist in San Diego, California. He has worked on many of the nation's top endurance athletes, and his ChekPoint sports medicine updates will occur throughout the book.

   As a massage therapist, I have learned to appreciate athletes who are willing to help themselves. They are injured less often and recover more quickly when they are injured than athletes who don't help themselves. Self-massage is an easily learned skill that requires only a few minutes of time to make a difference. The only tools you need are your hands and some type of massage oil (cold, compressed peanut oil or even Vaseline

Massage therapist Paul Chek.

works well). Hot water and soap work well too. A great place to self-massage is in the bathtub. Not only do you get the benefits of the hot water, but you also can get clean at the same time.

   The way to start is to put the muscle group to be worked in a relaxed position that is accessible to one or both hands. For a calf muscle, for instance, you can rest your foot on the edge of the tub near the tap and lean forward to reach it. First soap the

Self-massage: once the muscle is warmed up, you can begin using deep strokes to remove any adhesions or knots and to break up any fibrous scar tissue.

calf, then begin with effleurage (long, firm, open-handed strokes) from the heel to the back of the knee. When not in the tub the same principle applies—just use a little oil or even baby powder.

These strokes can vary in pressure from light and fast to slow and firm. The purpose of effleurage is to warm the muscles in preparation for the therapeutic strokes and to move large amounts of blood for an almost washing effect. Effleurage should be done for several strokes until the skin is warm, or approximately one to three minutes. *To keep from damaging the valves within the veins, these strokes should always be done toward the heart.*

The next stroke will be petrissage, which is performed by taking alternate handfuls of tissue and lifting and twisting them in a kneading fashion. Petrissage squeezes the muscle, causing a good hyperemia (increased blood flow to the part being worked) and improving elasticity and contractility. This stroke should be done for at least three forward and backward passes of a muscle or muscle group.

Next, broad cross-fiber friction can be done by sweeping the thumb or fingers at a 90-degree angle to the grain of the muscle with moderate pressure. The purpose of this stroke is to feel for lumps or bundles of tissue that may be tight or stuck together and to tease them apart. The areas that do not come apart can be further loosened by focusing on a knot or tight spot and holding firm, deep pressure on it for 10 to 60 seconds, followed by a more focused and deeper transverse friction.

This technique is not too pleasurable to administer to oneself, but if you feel pain I doubt you'll overdo it. The transition from stroke to stroke can be made with a few passes of effleurage or a little jostling to encourage a relaxed state.

Massage warms the muscles, dilates the capillaries, encourages blood flow, increases oxygen and nutrient supply, and removes metabolic (by-product of metabolism) and catabolic (harmful to tissue) waste products, which greatly reduce recovery time. The end result of this fun in the tub is the facilitation of a greater work load and the reduction of aches and pains as well as injury prevention for the athlete.

Self-massage can be administered at any time, although I feel it is best used in the evening of any hard workout day. It is best to get the tissue loosened and separated as well as cleaned out with fresh blood right away to speed recovery. Performing this treatment on the hard days is most effective, since most training programs follow hard days with easy days. This is quite beneficial to the recovery process.

INDOOR TURBO TRAINING WORKOUT

The turbo trainer is a valuable tool for the biathelete. On some wind-training devices you need to take the front wheel off your bike. Others accommodate the whole bicycle. In either case, a turbo trainer will make efficient use of your limited training time. Some athletes, like Bob Macy, a top 40-year-old biathlete from San Diego, spend nearly 75 percent of their total cycling training time on the turbo trainer, either watching television, listening to music on their headphones, or studying their cycling form in the mirror.

For the novice, cycling indoors is safer with fewer distractions than cycling on the roads. Of course, riding a bicycle that doesn't move *is* monotonous. That's why I've incorporated Dan Rock's turbo-training program (below) into my schedule. It forces me to use all the gears and provides an opportunity for me to work on my pedaling skills at the same time. I think you'll like it too.

This is the indoor wind trainer with the Spin Coach attachment.

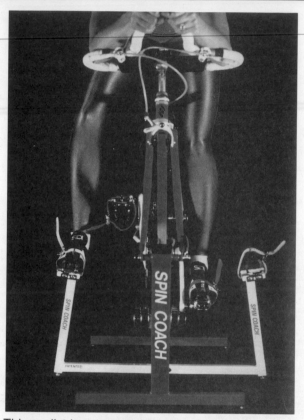

This cyclist is set up to ride with one leg at a time. Isolated leg training will help make your cycling stroke smoother and more efficient.

This is an indoor workout you can complete in about 40 minutes.

In the front sprockets of your bicycle you have a large chain ring (LCR) and a small chain ring (SCR). Your rear cluster will have six or seven gears. Your first gear is low and it is closest to your wheel. It probably has a 21- or 23-tooth cog. Your sixth or seventh gear is the farthest gear from the wheel and probably has a 13-tooth cog.

1. Warm-up
   (five minutes)

   SCR in front, second or first gear in back. Build RPMs to 90.

2. Increase warm-up
   (five minutes)

   SCR in front, second and third gears in back (alternate 30 seconds each).
   Raise RPMs to 100.

3. Getting ready for speed work
   (five minutes)

   Alternate 20-second fast spins in SCR, fourth or fifth gear with 40-second spins in SCR, second or third gear.

4. Solid repeats
   Number 1

   Five minutes LCR in the front, fourth gear in the back, 15-tooth or 17-tooth cog. Two minutes' recovery time: SCR, second or third gear, 17-tooth or 19-tooth cog.

   Number 2

   Five minutes LCR, fourth gear, 15-tooth or 17-tooth cog. Two minutes' recovery time: SCR, second or third gear, 17-tooth or 19-tooth cog.

Note: when working on the turbo trainer, I try to have a block-type cluster with one-tooth increments. Sometimes only a two-tooth reduction in cog size will raise your heart rate 10 beats per minute!

Number 3

Five minutes LCR, fourth gear, 15-tooth or 17-tooth cog. Two minutes' recovery time: SCR, second or third gear, 17-tooth or 19-tooth cog.

5. Cool-down

You're almost done. Finish your workout with three minutes of easy riding, SCR, second or third gear, followed by ten 15-second sprints with 45 to 50 seconds of rest in between each sprint. Sprints should be done as fast as possible in LCR, fourth or fifth gear. You should get your heart rate up to around 150. Don't sprint past the point of losing form or technique. Be smooth, quick, fast, *and* controlled. Maybe only 10 seconds of sprinting at 120 RPMs is enough.

6. Isolated leg training

Now is a good time to do some isolated leg training with The Spin Coach. This device attaches to your trainer and allows you to rest one leg on it while pedaling with the other. I do 20 seconds SCR first or second gear at 100 RPM. Try to spin nice, smooth, round circles. Then 40 seconds normal riding. Then 20 seconds with the other leg, followed by 40 seconds with both legs. Repeat 5–10 times with each leg.

7. Final cool-down

Follow your last sprint with a two-to-four minute LCR spin, 15-tooth cog, and finally, a five-minute cool-down, reducing gears as you go.

Ladder Work

Indoor training can get monotonous, so I try to incorporate ladder work into my training as an alternative to solid repeats. Below, I've provided what I think is a challenging ladder workout.

One minute LCR, fourth or fifth gear, 15-tooth or 17-tooth cog.	Ride hard.
One minute SCR, second or third gear, 17-tooth or 19-tooth cog.	Ride easy.
Two minutes LCR, fourth or fifth gear, 15-tooth or 17-tooth cog.	Ride hard.
One minute SCR, second or third gear, 17-tooth or 19-tooth cog.	Ride easy.
Three minutes LCR, third or fourth gear, 15-tooth or 17-tooth cog.	Ride hard.
One minute SCR, second or third gear, 17-tooth or 19-tooth cog.	Ride easy.
Four minutes LCR, third or fourth gear, 15-tooth or 17-tooth cog.	Ride hard.
One minute SCR, second or third gear, 17-tooth or 19-tooth cog.	Ride easy.
Five minutes LCR, third or fourth gear, 15-tooth or 17-tooth cog.	Ride hard.
One minute SCR, second or third gear, 17-tooth or 19-tooth cog.	Ride easy.

You can also change gear ratios within a ladder workout; for example: six minutes on LCR, one minute on SCR.

First repeat
(six minutes hard): four minutes LCR, third gear
two minutes LCR, fourth gear
one minute recovery, SCR

Second repeat
(six minutes hard): three minutes LCR, third gear
two minutes LCR, fourth gear
one minute LCR, fifth gear
one minute recovery, SCR

Third repeat
(six minutes hard): two minutes LCR, third gear
two minutes LCR, fourth gear
two minutes LCR, fifth gear
one minute recovery, SCR

Fourth repeat
(six minutes hard): one minute LCR, third gear
two minutes LCR, fourth gear
two minutes LCR, fifth gear
one minute LCR, sixth gear
one minute recovery, SCR

Fifth repeat
(six minutes hard): two minutes LCR, fourth gear
two minutes LCR, fifth gear
one minute LCR, sixth gear
one minute LCR, fifth gear
one minute recovery, SCR

Race-Course Simulation

You won't want to try race-course simulation until you've worked out steadily for at least one month. Break the course into 10-minute segments. Ride 10 minutes hard, two minutes easy.

First repeat: 10 minutes LCR, third gear
                   two minutes SCR
Second repeat: 10 minutes LCR, fourth gear
                   two minutes SCR
Third repeat: two minutes LCR, fourth gear
                   two minutes LCR, third gear
                   two minutes LCR, fourth gear
                   two minutes LCR, third gear
                   two minutes SCR

To simulate downhills, use lower gears. For uphills, go into higher gears.

3
RUNNING

If you are a first-time runner, this chapter is not just important; it's essential. Many people think they can put on their five-year-old sneakers and their cutoffs and head out the door with no problems. But like anything else, running takes practice, and running correctly takes work. If you learn the proper technique early, you'll save yourself valuable time and injury later on.

IF THE SHOE FITS . . .

Author and runner Dr. George Sheehan says that finding the right running shoe is like finding the right mate. Sheehan is right. Running shoes have become quite a science—at first glance, an unfathomable science. Don't despair. Remember a few basics, find a competent salesperson, ask a few of the right questions, and with a little luck you'll find yourself married to the shoes that are right for you.

The first and most important thing to remember is that there is a shoe out there that is perfectly suited to you. Because technology has taken the running shoe so far,

The keys to a good running shoe are fit, support, and performance. Everybody's feet are a little bit different, so go to a reputable retail outlet to make sure that you are fitted properly.

Photo courtesy of Avia

there are literally hundreds of variations aimed to suit thousands of runners. Never have the choices been so great. Your job is to take advantage of these choices.

A word of caution: what is right for someone else isn't necessarily right for you. This is probably the beginning shoe buyer's (and many veterans') biggest mistake. Your next-door neighbor swears by a particular brand; this shoe, she tells you, is the only choice. She's tried the others, and now she's going to save you injuries and wasted time. She's found the perfect shoe. Great for her, but not for you. Don't, if you'll pardon the pun, try to fill your neighbor's shoes.

If your neighbor doesn't trip you up, your local shoe-store salesman may. He too is infatuated with the shoe he is using at the moment. Well-meaning but uninformed, he pushes it on you. His advice is even more alluring because as a running-shoe salesman he has some credibility. He is supposed to be knowledgeable. If he pushes what he's wearing, he isn't. Thank him and walk out before you end up spending $100 on a shoe you don't need.

A little bit of knowledge can go a long way. Dr. Richard Schuster, a widely respected sports podiatrist (Sheehan calls him the Ted Williams of sports podiatrists), has a number

On the downhills, try to stay relaxed and
just let yourself go.

of suggestions for running-shoe buyers. Schuster's practical,
simple advice will go a long way toward ensuring you end
up in the right pair of shoes.

First, when you are just getting started, Schuster recommends that you go for your first few runs in the knockabout
running shoes you are wearing now. See how they feel. Are
they too heavy? Do they feel inflexible? Do they pinch your
toes when you run? These early discoveries provide you
with an economical starting point—you can decide what
you like and don't like without buying a new pair of shoes.

Photo by Lois Schwartz

People used to say that the only way to become a great runner was to just run. The performances by biathletes and triathletes in running events around the country have changed that theory. Cross-training is the key that makes you stronger and ultimately faster. Here is Scott Tinley (right) at the La Jolla Half Marathon outside of San Diego. He battled it out for the lead with full-time runner Sean Evans (left) of Orange County, California. Evans eventually won the race.

Once you're committed to buying a new pair of running shoes, there are a few things you should know. First, pay no attention to size. What you wear in street shoes (or running shoes for that matter) is at best a starting point. Many running shoes are made in foreign countries where sizing is measured in completely different dimensions. Even shoes with familiar measurements do not by any means guarantee an exact fit. In fact, two pairs of shoes in the exact same model and size may still be slightly different. Don't just pick a box off the shelf and walk out the door. Have the salesperson fit you, then see how the shoe feels. You want a shoe that's snug in the back, flexible at the ball, and has about a half-inch space between your longest toe and the end of the shoe.

Why these criteria? First let's talk about snugness in the back of the running shoe. Almost all running shoes made today have a heel counter, a band (sometimes plastic, sometimes another material) that cups the heel and may run as far forward as the middle of the shoe. The heel counter holds the heel in place, keeping it from wandering from side to side and bringing on any number of injuries when your feet strike the ground 10,000 times each mile you run. A large heel counter is not necessarily a good one. The best test here, says Schuster, is to simply pick up the shoe and give the counter a squeeze. It should resist squeezing; if it feels too flabby, it will not provide the support you need. Weak heel counters can also shorten the lifespan of the shoe—if you don't twist your ankle first.

Moving to the ball of your foot, Schuster recommends that the fit here be loose enough so that you can pinch a small bit of the shoe's upper material between your fingers. The ball of the foot encompasses a major system of joints, and these joints need flexibility. Along with pinching, you can also test a running shoe's all-important give in the ball by grabbing the shoe by the toe and flexing it back. There should be flexibility at the ball, which is the widest part of the shoe.

Finding out whether there is enough space between your toes and the end of the shoe is not a cut-and-dried process. Everyone's feet elongate when they run, which is why Schuster recommends a half-inch gap. However, some runners' feet elongate more than others', and the half-inch space is only a general rule of thumb. If your toenails start turning black or your feet burn and tingle when you run, your shoe may be too small. Also (and this may seem ridiculously commonsensical, but many people forget), make sure you test the shoe's fit while standing up. Your body weight makes your foot elongate, and a half-inch gap when you are seated will quickly disappear as soon as you stand.

Once you find a shoe that seems to fit, Schuster recommends that you jog around the store. The foot you run with is a far different foot from the one you walk with, and the only way you will get a feel for how a running shoe performs is to run in it. Most good running-shoe stores will allow you to take a spin, and a competent salesperson will run behind you, watching for peculiarities in gait that may require a particular shoe.

There are a few other things to look for in new shoes. New shoes should stand perfectly straight when placed on a table and viewed from the back. Also (and this is particularly important), look at the shoe's *last,* or general outline. According to Schuster, up to 80 percent of all runners need what is called a straight last. The test to find a straight last is simple. Flip the shoe over and look at the bottom. If you have a hard time telling the left shoe from the right, then you're probably looking at a straight-last shoe, and odds are the straight last is right for you. If you don't fall into the majority, you may need a curved last, a shoe bottom that is shaped like a comma. There's really no need, however, to get too bogged down with these and the thousand other nuances that make up a running shoe. A knowledgeable salesperson will be able to take a look at your foot and tell you whether you need a straight last or a curved last.

The best way to learn pace and technique is to train and race with other people. Focusing on their form will help yours.

Photo by Lois Schwartz

Photo by Bob Babbitt

Running with someone else often helps you focus on your form. These two women are top road racers Liz Baker (left) and Monica Joyce (right). They use each other's energy to go faster than they would on their own.

Schuster also warns beginners to stay away from shoes that are light and soft. If a shoe feels soft in the store, it will be much too soft when you run. Soft, light shoes introduce an element of instability that is dangerous unless you have a nearly flawless gait. Experienced runners can sometimes successfully use such shoes, but even they choose only to race in them, relying on heavier (we're talking ounces here), sturdier shoes for training.

A final point regarding light shoes: many have a cut-out under the arch. This, says Schuster, is a no-no. Support has been removed from the shoe where it is needed most. Your arch depresses when you run, and arch supports, says Schuster, are crucial. Do not buy a shoe without full arch support. If you have a question regarding arch support, ask the salesperson.

Now the big question: how much is all of this going to cost? It depends on whom you talk to, but most experts agree that you don't have to spend an arm and a leg for a good pair of running shoes. In fact, says Schuster, you may even get lucky and find that the shoe best suited to you costs as little as $30. The important thing to remember is that the most expensive shoe is not necessarily the right shoe for you. Expect to spend between $40 and $60 for a good pair of running shoes, says Schuster, but don't judge a shoe by its price.

Armed with the essentials, you are now better equipped to shop around. However, a little bit of knowledge can be a dangerous thing. Don't assume you know it all; unless you're a biomechanic or a sports podiatrist, chances are you don't. Find a running-shoe store with knowledgeable sales-people, the crucial link between you and the perfect shoe. Remember my earlier advice: if a salesman begins raving about the shoes he's been using or grabs a box out of the stack and guarantees it's right for you, get up and get out.

You can be of some help in the process of finding the right shoe. If you've already been running, bring in a list of the shoes that worked well for you in the past. This will give the salesperson a good idea of where to start and eliminate a lot of the searching. Your old shoes can also act as a road map. By carefully examining where your shoes are worn, a competent salesperson can see any irregularities in your running form and fit you with a new shoe that will compensate for those irregularities. Also, don't forget to ask the salesperson how the new shoe ages. Some shoes wear better than others, and a knowledgeable (and honest) sales-person will be able to tell you how well a shoe holds up under real-world wear and tear.

When you finally decide on a pair of shoes, you'll be thrilled and excited, primed to dash out the door. Don't. Walk around in the shoes first, preferably for a few days. New running shoes are like new jeans—they need to be worn in. Don't throw them in the washer, and don't run a marathon in them either. Walk around the block, pad around your house. Running in just-off-the-shelf shoes invites blisters at best, disaster at worst.

It's important to realize that running shoes, even the most

Photo by Lois Schwartz

This is Arturo Barrios showing his perfect form. Take a good look at Barrios and the next time you run, try to remember how fast and light he looks. When you get tired it helps to visualize the smoothest runner you've ever seen. Believe it or not, visualization can help you maintain your form.

Photo by Lois Schwartz

How important is full leg extension when you run? Take a look at the stride of top Canadian runner Sue Berenda. You can tell that she also makes great use of her arms.

perfectly suited, are not a cure-all. Running, points out Schuster, is not natural to humans. Anyone who runs knows that injuries are part of the game. Unfortunately, just as "perfect" shoes are often mistakenly viewed as a panacea, "lousy" shoes are often used as a scapegoat. Toe-nail injuries may mean your shoes are too small, but shin splints, back pains, or muscle pulls could be caused by any number of things from poor running form to no warm-up. If problems persist, don't continue to throw out shoe after shoe; use that money to see a professional. The idea is to be on the road, not in the waiting room.

RUNNING TECHNIQUE

Are you a first-time runner? If you are, here are a few things to think about after you've purchased your first pair of running shoes.

Posture

Think tall. Stay upright when you run, not bent over like someone looking for change on the ground.

Photo by Lois Schwartz

Running the trails is a good way to stay healthy and build strength.

Foot Strike

You want your feet to skim the ground. Think "soft," and pretend that you are running on eggshells. You want to think about just touching down. After you start to feel comfortable with that, think about touching and reaching, sort of like a trotting horse. Joggers are notorious for burying their feet when they land, rather than reaching and putting their feet out in front of them.

Skipping Drill

Ted Van Arsdale, one of the premier running coaches in southern California, likes to have his new students start out with skipping drills to learn how to run correctly, and I think the drills can benefit you too. These drills consist of

As a high school cross-country runner, I won the league championships for three straight years at Wilson High School.

I'm very proud of my high school running career.
I loved every minute of it.

skipping short distances using the same skipping motion
you may have used when you were a kid. When a jogger
buries her foot rather than reaching out, she will eventually
develop hamstring or quadricep pain.

The idea of the skipping drills is to get you to keep your
head up and your foot out. First do five sets of 40-to-50-yard
skipping drills. Then do another five sets of 50 yards in an
easy jog. On the first jog, work on staying tall. On number
two, concentrate on keeping your arms low and relaxed,
your shoulders relaxed, and your elbow joints opened up.
The idea behind a relaxed upper body is that any extra
energy used to keep the upper body tense does absolutely
nothing to help the legs turn over faster. So relax! On
number three, your head is tall, arms are swinging, and

hands are loose, like you're holding a potato chip between your thumb and first finger. Remember to bring your knees up high. On number four, concentrate on the knee lift, then drop your heel down for the foot strike, roll from the heel to the ball of the foot, and push off. That will take the vertical bounce out of your stride. Vertical bounce is another waste of energy. The idea is to go forward, not up. Again, think about skimming over the ground.

More Advanced Drills

When you skip, your right knee and left arm should come up at the same time, as should your left knee and right arm. When your leg and arm come up, cock your ankle and wrist up before hitting the ground. Then follow through and push back. Van Arsdale will take his beginners and move them from skipping drills to the stairs to help reinforce what the runners have just learned. The stairs teach them to take short steps and to touch down softly on each and every stair. You can hear if you start to pound your foot strike, and you can tell whether one foot is pounding more than the other.

Think when you run. There's more to it than putting one foot in front of the other. Sometimes it's hard to focus on form and technique when you are running the roads and dodging cars and trucks. That's where the track comes in handy. It's the best place to think about what you're doing. Think smooth, think light, and most of all . . . think *fast*!

CHEKPOINT: STRETCHING by Paul Chek

As a biathlete you are a special breed of athlete. In your quest for improved performance you will take on all the stresses of both the runner and the cyclist. When combining these two leg-dominant sports, good stress management and preventive maintenance are crucial to success. Stretching is an important form of cost-free preventive maintenance that can make the difference for a race day or a race season. Unless you are very wealthy and can afford a trained therapist to work on you every day, stretching is a valuable tool for identifying problem areas. As a natural form of self-maintenance, it is an excellent way to warm up or cool down after any exercise session.

I can tell you from experience that someone who doesn't stretch is much more susceptible to injury than someone who has the discipline to find the time for it. There is a direct correlation between injured athletes and poor stretching habits. If you are finding yourself constantly pressed for time, I suggest warming up by doing your sporting event at a greatly reduced intensity until a sweat has developed. It is much more productive to go home and stretch properly after the workout. This gives you the time to relax and devote yourself to the maintenance work at hand. You're also more likely to do a better job staying flexible.

Stretch as shown until your head is at a 45-degree angle.

Why Stretch?

1. Stretching is an excellent way to identify problem areas. Hard exercise causes microtrauma to muscles and tendons. With repetition this leads to shortening of the soft tissues. If there is an area damaged beyond what the body can tolerate, the affected and surrounding muscles respond with a spasm in order to protect the area. When this process begins, there is reduced range of motion of the involved joints. This will result in such

Hamstring stretch. Increase stretch from this position by leaning your upper body toward your leg. Put your hands on your leg if you can't reach your foot. Stretch one hamstring, then the other.

This stretch is for the medial hamstrings. To increase the stretch, bring your chest as close to your leg as possible.

This is for the upper calf. Keeping your knee locked, lean into the stretch, bringing your whole leg closer to your foot. Another stretch for the calf using this same position is done by bringing your shin closer to your foot with your knee bent. Never let the stretch go as low as the Achilles tendon. Again, work one calf muscle, then the other.

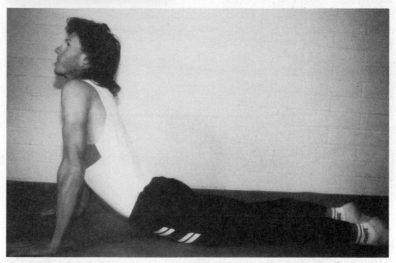

Abdominal stretch. Once in the position pictured, the stretch can be increased by relaxing your stomach and filling your belly with air. By rotating from the trunk in either direction, you will stretch your external obliques as well.

things as tight hamstrings or quadriceps, common problems for the biathlete. With this in mind, you can see how stretching will help you identify problem areas. For instance, if you find that your right hamstring is always much tighter than your left, you may be developing an overuse injury. Or if it is painful to stretch the hamstring, then it may be torn, and you should seek help from a sports-injury specialist.

Groin and hamstring stretch. Reach slowly between your legs. Try to keep your back flat. Once you feel a stretch in this position, move your trunk toward either leg to change muscle groups.

Rectus femoris stretch. To increase the stretch from this position, bring your pelvis down toward the ground.

2. Avoiding muscle damage is another reason to stretch regularly. Muscles tear when the associated joint is pushed beyond the available range of motion. An athlete with poor stretching habits has an available range of motion that is likely to be substantially less than it could be. For example, if your hamstrings (hip extensors and knee flexors) are tight, it is likely that you could tear a muscle when running downhill in training or racing. A muscle tear is simply an overstretch. This injury can be prevented by maintaining optimum flexibility.

3. Adhesion, scarring, and microtrauma are all muscle and tendon problems that the biathlete has to contend with at one time or another. In general, these are all the result of a less than adequate work/rest ratio. Regular stretching combats the formation of adhesions (clumping of muscle fibers) and scar tissue as well as promotes the healing of microtrauma (microscopic tears) by keeping the muscle at its natural resting length. As muscles are worked they tend to shorten. This is evident the day after a microtrauma because moving the muscle becomes painful. If the damage is bad enough the muscle will spasm in an attempt to splint off the area. This is the body's survival reflex, an attempt to get you to rest the muscle. This is very common during the last

Glutes stretch. To get the maximum stretch from this position, pull your foot toward your chest.

Groin stretch. Using your feet as an anchor point, increase the stretch by adding downward pressure with your forearms on your shins.

run of a biathlon. Your calves have endured the first run and a bike ride; now you're dehydrated and tired and asking the muscles to perform under adverse conditions. This protective reaction by the body usually begins with a mighty cramping of the upper portion of your calves.

A good stretching program keeps the muscle tissue supple, which promotes circulation and in turn results in reduced recovery time.

An athlete with less than ideal flexibility should strive to achieve good flexibility and then maintain it. Once you have achieved good flexibility, maintaining it is much less effort.

How to Stretch

Most athletes avoid stretching because they say it hurts. If you're stretching properly, however, you should not be feeling any pain.

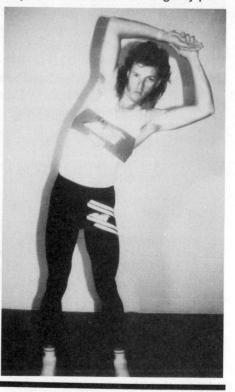

Latissimus dorsi and quadratus lumarum stretch. When doing this stretch it is important to keep the arm on the side being stretched in line with your ear. You can move your hips forward and backward to change the stretch angle.

Each muscle is loaded with little devices called spindle cells. These special muscle fibers constantly monitor the length of a muscle. When you stretch into the pain zone these special muscle fibers send a message to the brain warning it of an injury about to happen. This in turn triggers a protective response by the body called the stretch reflex. When the stretch reflex is activated the body strongly contracts all the muscles surrounding the involved joints to stabilize them and prevent further movement. You will know when this reflex has been activated because all the muscles in the area of the joint you're stretching will get very tight. At this point all you're doing is spending time in pain for no reason.

When you're ready to stretch, start by putting on some loose clothing, preferably after a jacuzzi or hot shower. To begin:

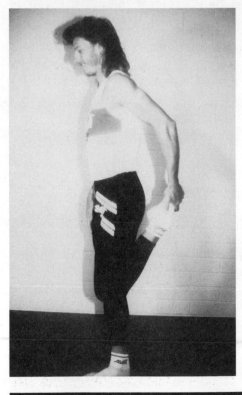

Quadriceps stretch. The closer your behind gets to your foot, the better the stretch.

1. Apply the stretch force in a slow, sustained manner. Take the joint to the point of tightness and then move just slightly beyond.

- The force must be enough to place tension on the soft tissue structures but not so great as to cause pain or injure the structures.
- Avoid ballistic stretching. Do not bounce the extremity at the end of the range, which will facilitate the stretch reflex and cause a reflex contraction of the muscles being stretched. Ballistic stretching tends to cause the greatest amount of trauma and injury to tissues.
- In the stretched position, you should experience a sense of pulling or tightness of the structures being stretched *but not pain*.

2. Hold this stretched position for at least 15 to 30 seconds or longer. This minimizes the stretch reflex.

- During this time tension in the tissues should slowly decrease.
- When tension decreases, move the extremity or joint a little farther.
- Gradually release the stretch force.

Each stretch should be done at least two times per stretching session.

Bibliography

Anderson, Bob. *Stretching*. Bolinas, CA: Shelter Publications, 1980.

Day, Robert W. "Improving Flexibility: Techniques and Rationale," *Sports Massage Journal*, Spring 1987.

Kisner, Carolyn and Lyn Allen Colby. *Therapeutic Exercise: Foundations and Techniques*. Philadelphia: Davis Company, 1985.

4
PUTTING IT ALL TOGETHER: A 12-WEEK TRAINING PROGRAM

OK, you've bought a pair of running shoes, and you have all the other paraphernalia that you'll need while training. You've ridden indoors for a few weeks and casually around the neighborhood for a few more. Our goal is to get you ready for the most popular of all biathlons, the 5K run/30K bike/5K run events that Coors Light is sponsoring all around the country. Because of the distances, we will keep the mileage relatively low, and in about 12 weeks, you will be adequately prepared to not only do your first biathlon but also to do well.

TRAINING ON THE BIKE

When you mount your bike for the first time, you'll notice that it has 10, 12, or 14 gears. There are two sprockets on the front, usually one with 53 teeth and the other with 42, plus five, six, or seven sprockets on the back, ranging from 13 teeth to 23 teeth. The reason for having different gears is fairly simple. If you can maintain the same physical effort (roughly 80 percent of your maximum) throughout the ride

Photo by Lois Schwartz

When taking a turn, take a hint from top road racer Bunki Bankaitis-Davis. Choose your line and lean into it.

and compensate for uphills and downhills with your gears, the bicycle becomes a helpful partner because it is doing most of the work. Obviously, your revolutions per minute (RPMs) will decrease as you climb steep hills, but by using your gears correctly you will find that whether you're climbing or enjoying a steep downhill, the work you're doing is basically the same.

If you feel like your cadence is slowing down even though the road looks flat, shift into an easier gear. The natural tendency is to stay in the same gear and look down to see if the tires are flat or if the brakes are rubbing. Hills can be deceptive. Even a slight change in the grade or even in the force or direction of the wind can make pedaling more difficult. When in doubt, shift. You always want to feel like you are in complete control of the gear you are using.

A good way to gauge whether you are being efficient on the bike is to use a heart monitor when you ride. A heart monitor consists of a strap with a sensor on it that goes across your chest. A large watch that displays and records your heart rate is worn on your wrist. By examining your heart rate you can monitor your effort as the terrain changes.

Momentum

Using the gears correctly will help you maintain momentum as you go to bigger and harder gears on the downhills and easier gears on the uphills. The goal of cycling is to learn how to control that momentum. The more you are on your bike, the easier it will be to develop a feel for proper momentum.

Cornering

As you ride around town, every once in a while you'll have to turn right or left. If there's no traffic around, you'll want to take the same line a race car would take. Swing wide, cut in tight around the turn, and swing wide again. If it's a right turn, you'll want to lift up the right foot to the top of the pedal stroke and point the right knee into the turn as you lean into it. That way your pedal won't scrape the ground as you make the turn. Try to visualize your line through the turn as you approach the corner.

Maintaining That Line

A common mistake most rookies tend to make is to look over their left shoulder to check traffic before changing lanes or riding around debris in the road. They won't notice that their bicycle is drifting to the left at the same time. For safety's sake, it's important to maintain your line and not drift into traffic. It's a good idea to wear a small rearview mirror on your helmet so you know at all times who and what is behind you.

Power Trips

For some reason, I've found that most runners are able to pick up bike-handling skills fairly quickly. It probably comes from a runner's knowledge of how to hang onto form while moving fast. The one aspect of cycling that does not come as quickly to runners, however, is power. Although spinning and establishing high revolutions per minute are important, the ability to move fast is what will make or break your race.

It's amazing to me that the same runners who know how important intervals and fartleks (alternating hard/easy/hard intervals in a continuous run) are tend to ignore the same type of speed work on the bike. One day per week I'll do a power ride over an undulating course with moderately steep hills. It's important that the hills aren't too steep because you'll want to be able to stay seated all the way to the top. Instead of using the small chain ring sprocket in the front, use the big sprocket and the 17 in the back. Start out at a moderate speed at the bottom, and then increase your effort and speed as you approach the top. Don't shift gears, and keep your body relaxed. That means no tugging on the handlebars! If you ride the aerodynamic bars, you should have your hands up near the pads. You don't want to be extended or lying down over the bars. Concentrate on turning circles, on bringing your foot and pedal over the top, and on breathing. This is a great workout. Remember to increase your momentum as you go.

Short, Steep Hills

This is another great way to increase your power. When I hit a short, steep hill during my power day, instead of downshifting to an easier gear, I'll stand up and punch over the top. When you get out of the saddle, try not to move your bike more than 5 percent to the right or left. Studies have shown that any more than 5 percent is wasted motion.

Less Mileage, More Quality

I have a tendency to ride a lot of miles, but I know I don't
need to. Joel Thompson, one of my fiercest competitors,
rides only 150–170 miles per week. Remember, you're training to do only an 18-to-20-mile bike ride. You don't need to
do 60-, 70-, or 80-mile rides. Sure, you'll improve your
endurance, but who cares how far you can go? The idea is to
go fast, to develop speed *and* endurance. A lot of riders just
put miles on their bikes. Don't. If you look at the athletes
who are doing really well on the bike in the multisport
world—Mike Pigg, Joel Thompson, and me—what do you
think we all have in common? Speed and power on the
bike.

YOUR SPECIFIC TRAINING PROGRAM

Now it's time to start shaping a specific training program.
Take your bike out and make sure you have at least one spare
tire and a frame pump along with a patch kit for flats. The
key here is not to overdo it. Remember, undertrain and be
healthy . . . overtrain and be hurt. The following program
is 12 weeks long—adequate time to prepare you for your
first race.

Week 1

Week 1 Schedule
Monday: ride 15 miles
Tuesday: run 4 miles
Wednesday: off
Thursday: ride 15 miles
Friday: run 4 miles
Saturday: off
Sunday: ride 10 miles, run 3 miles
Totals: ride 40 miles, run 11 miles

Day 1 (Monday)   Your first official I'm-getting-ready-
for-a-race workout should be a 15-mile ride. Time yourself,
so that in the future weeks you can compare your time as it

improves. Put into practice what you've learned while turbo training and cruising the neighborhood. Concentrate on spinning circles, using a gear that you can control, and staying smooth and comfortable. Don't forget to breathe. Your hands should be relaxed on the handlebars, and your legs should feel invisible, as if they're doing all the work themselves.

Day 2 (Tuesday)   Your first run is a four-miler. I remember a coach once telling me to pretend I was running on a huge ball. To stay on top of it, I had to try to push back each time a foot hit the ground. I feel this visualization helps with follow-through in the running stride. Just as in cycling, try to keep your legs and arms relaxed. Be aware of your stride. Visualize the smoothest runner you've ever seen and try to emulate that person.

Day 3 (Wednesday)   This is your day off. Do anything you want—just don't ride or run!

Day 4 (Thursday)   The same as Day 1, 15 easy miles on the bike. Try out all the gears and develop a feel for your brakes.

Day 5 (Friday)   Repeat Day 2, another four-miler through the neighborhood. Reach with your arms; you're light and fast!

Day 6 (Saturday)   Another day off. Spend time with your family, mow the lawn, or rake the leaves. Rest up and drink plenty of fluids. Tomorrow will be your first multisport workout.

Day 7 (Sunday)   Start out with a 10-mile ride, again staying smooth and concentrating on turning perfect circles with your feet. On the hills pretend there is a brick on your foot during the upstroke and keep your foot flat so the brick doesn't fall off. This will help you focus on pulling up correctly. Toward the end of the ride, make sure you are well hydrated. Spin in an easy gear during the last mile or two, dismount, then change quickly into your running gear for a three-mile run. At first your legs will feel heavy, but they'll loosen up after about a half mile. Notice where you are tight, and be aware of any part of your body that is experiencing more than just a little discomfort. If you have pain in your knees, hips, neck, or back, you should consider taking your bike in to see that it is set up correctly. Sometimes it takes a while to fine-tune your position.

After you finish, lie on the grass and stretch out. Make sure you drink lots of water.

Congratulations! You have finished your first week of training and are now a full-fledged biathlete. Ten weeks from now you'll make it official.

Week 2

Week 2 Schedule
Monday: ride 15 miles
Tuesday: run 4 miles
Wednesday: off
Thursday: ride 15 miles
Friday: run 4 miles
Saturday: off
Sunday: ride 10 miles, run 3 miles
_____
Totals: ride 40 miles, run 11 miles

No matter how excited you are about Sunday's performance, Monday of your second week should still be just a 15-mile ride. (Since 99 percent of all biathletes are working folks, my program is set up with the weekend warrior in mind.) Harder, longer workouts on the weekends are balanced with shorter, easier days on Fridays and Mondays. The rest of this week should be the same as week one: a four-mile run on Tuesday, off on Wednesday, another 15-mile ride on Thursday, a four-mile run on Friday, and off again on Saturday. Try to rest well on Saturday of your second week. Remember, you have added a lot of physical stress to your life in the past two weeks, and this second Sunday is your second practice biathlon. Relax and enjoy it.

Week 3

Week 3 Schedule

Monday: ride 15 miles
Tuesday: run 6 miles
Wednesday: off
Thursday: ride 15 miles
Friday: run 6 miles
Saturday: off
Sunday: run 2 miles, ride 10 miles, run 2 miles

Totals: ride 40 miles, run 16 miles

On Monday you're going to go 15 miles again, but this time ride a little bit harder. Keep track of your time on the bike. Your goal this week is to better your time from Week 1. On Tuesday run six miles instead of four. This run is meant to be easy. If you're training intelligently, you will be alternating hard days with easy days. Since Monday was a hard ride, Tuesday will be an easy run. Wednesday will be off, Thursday is an easy 15-mile ride, and Friday, if your legs feel up to it, a hard six-mile run. And, of course, after any hard running effort, *stretch out*. Saturday is another day off.

On Sunday you'll be doing your first run-bike-run, a two-mile run followed by a 10-mile bike ride followed by another two-mile run. Take the first run a bit slower than your 10K pace. Don't overdo it! You still have to ride 10 miles and then come back and run one more time. If you can, set up a transition area in front of your house or in the backyard. I know I looked pretty foolish, but I used to set up a transition area in front of my house and just practice putting my bike gear on and taking it off. Then I'd practice riding in, putting my running gear on, and heading out again. Anyhow, as long as you're doing run-bike-run training, go for the whole enchilada and practice transitions at the same time.

Did your legs feel different from the last time you did a combined workout? Remember, the wear and tear of train-

Photo by Lois Schwartz

This is Scott Molina, who taught me a lot about training and racing and how to deal with their ups and downs.

ing is cumulative. You never know when your body is going to say, "Hey, this is too much!" Stay tuned in. If something hurts, *back off*.

Week 4

Week 4 Schedule
Monday: ride 15 miles
Tuesday: run 6 miles
Wednesday: off
Thursday: ride 15 miles
Friday: run 6 miles
Saturday: off
Sunday: run 2 miles, ride 10 miles, run 2 miles
Totals: ride 40 miles, run 16 miles

Week 4 should be exactly the same as Week 3. No extra workouts!

Week 5

Week 5 Schedule
Monday: ride 20 miles
Tuesday: run 6 miles
Wednesday: off
Thursday: ride 20 miles
Friday: run 6 miles
Saturday: off
Sunday: run 3 miles, ride 15 miles, run 3 miles
Totals: ride 55 miles, run 18 miles

Monday increase your bike mileage to twenty miles, still easy. Tuesday run six miles, this time with a little speed play, or fartlek, thrown in. The first two miles should be easy, the middle two very fast, and the last two easy again. Wednesday is a day off, and Thursday is a hard 20-miler on the bike. Friday is an easy six-mile run, followed by another day off on Saturday. Sunday run three miles, ride 15, and run another three. Your legs will probably be fatigued at the end of the Sunday ride, but by now you should be used to running tired.

Week 6

Week 6 Schedule
Monday: ride 20 miles

Tuesday: run 6 miles
Wednesday: off
Thursday: ride 20 miles
Friday: run 6 miles
Saturday: off
Sunday: run 3 miles, ride 15 miles, run 3 miles
Totals: ride 55 miles, run 18 miles

Repeat Week 5. You'll probably notice that you are eating more than ever before. You are also burning up more calories than ever before! Make sure you supplement your training with stretching and abdominal work. And if you feel like doing something a little different, jump into a pool and do some laps just for fun. It's great for a change of pace.

Week 7

Week 7 Schedule
Monday: ride 10–15 miles, run 5 miles
Tuesday: ride 20 miles
Wednesday: run intervals
Thursday: ride 10 miles
Friday: off
Saturday: ride 20–25 miles, run 5 miles
Sunday: run 6–7 miles
Totals: ride 65–70 miles, run 22 miles

During Week 7 you will be adding some running workouts on cycling days and some cycling workouts on running days. You'll notice that all the hard rides are accompanied by easy runs and vice versa. Also, if the run is in the morning, the ride should be in the afternoon. The only combined workout you should be doing right now is on the weekend, either as a simulated race day or as the real thing.

Day 1 (Monday)   Monday is still a recovery day for you. Combine an easy 10–15 mile ride in the morning and a moderately paced five-mile run later in the day.

Day 2 (Tuesday)   This is your bike power day. Do a 20-mile ride using your big chain ring on the longer, gradual uphills. The idea is to build speed as you climb the hill. If you feel fatigued from your first ride-and-run workout the day before, don't push hard on the bike. Concentrate on your form, and think about bringing that foot over the top on each pedal stroke. No running today.

Day 3 (Wednesday)　No riding today. This is your first running interval day. Find a nice, flat, grassy area, and run about one easy mile to warm up. Next, mark off 100 yards and run some pick-ups. A pick-up is a 100-yard run on the track straightway, starting slow and "picking up" the pace until you're at full speed by the end of the 100 yards. Concentrate on your knee lift and use your arms as you run four 100-yard repeats. Start each one slowly and build to a faster pace during the last 50 yards. The purpose is to get you thinking about form and to get your body warmed up and ready to go. The workout for the day is five quarter-mile repeats with a 220 jog in between. You'll want to repeat your quarter-miles at a faster pace than race pace. For example, if you run a 44-minute 10K, you'll want to repeat your quarter-mile jaunts at 1:40, or 100 seconds per quarter mile. This means you'll be running the equivalent of a 6:40 mile broken into four quarters. After each quarter, run a 220 jog. The idea of intervals is to learn how to stay smooth and light on your feet while running faster than normal pace. You'll be able to maintain a faster pace on race day with little to no increase in effort. If you find you are out of breath during your intervals, then you are doing them too fast. The point is not to run one quarter mile at 80 seconds, two at 90, and then the last three over 100. All your repeats should be around 100 seconds. Develop a feel for pace. This will come in handy on race day. Eventually, you will be doing this workout on the track, but for right now it's important to ease into speed work, staying on soft surfaces.

Building endurance can be done without too much stress on the body. But speed is different. As top amateur Dan Rock once told me, speed kills. It's true. You need to be very careful when you start speed work because it's intoxicating.

The faster you go, the more you want to do. *Speed is not something to be trifled with.* If you work it into your training program in small doses, you will get fast and stay healthy. If not, you may get fast for a while, but I guarantee you won't stay healthy.

The basic premise of all training programs? Training is like building a pyramid. The foundation, or base, is the workouts you've been doing up until now. These workouts are sometimes called bricks, the physical effort you have to put out to create your training pyramid. The bigger the base of the pyramid, the higher the peak. Basically, that means that the bigger base you build, the faster you'll eventually be able to go. By following your training program and building a base, which includes that very important combined weekend workout, you're also building strength. When those factors are stable, you are then ready for speed. If you try to jump the gun and add too much too soon, your body won't be ready. But since you have followed our workouts to the letter so far, your first running interval workout should be a piece of cake!

After any type of interval workout, always warm down with at least an easy mile. Then stretch out well before going home. After heating yourself up, it's important to make sure you have cooled down sufficiently before getting in the car and driving home. Imagine this scenario: You've finished a hard interval session, but you're in a hurry and decide not to cool down or stretch. You hop in the car and drive home. When you get out of the car, your legs are like rubber. Take the time to take care of your body. Cool down and stretch out.

Day 4 (Thursday)   After that tough interval workout on Wednesday, Thursday is a short, fast ride day: a total of 10 miles with a warm-up of three miles, then a hard mile, followed by an easy three miles. The last three miles should be your warm-down. If your legs feel loose later in the day, try an easy two-mile run just to shake out the effects of yesterday's speed work.

Day 5 (Friday)   Friday is a day off. You've added a few multisport days this week, and Saturday will be another one. Eat well, drink lots of water, and Relax!

Day 6 (Saturday)   Saturday is a great day to ride with a group. Ride 20–25 miles and get used to riding with a pack. In cycling, the front rider is the one who breaks the wind and puts out the most effort. Find out what it feels like to lead the group, but make sure you don't end up performing a self-sacrifice. Many a novice rider will stay in the lead much longer than anyone else, surprised that they could possibly be leading this group of elite cyclists. You've been had. A *peloton,* or cycling pack, will sit behind any rider or riders who in their infinite wisdom have decided that they want to spend their morning pulling the pack. As the leader, you use 25 percent more energy than the riders behind you. Eventually, you will tire and be off the back.

Relax, take an appropriate turn up front (called a *pull*), and then drop back. Pack riding will help you develop a feeling for pace plus a much-needed ability to handle a bicycle in a crowd.

Again, remember that you are the student. Notice when the others shift their gears, how they work their bikes on the hills, and how they position themselves in the saddle. I've learned an incredible amount from participating in a group ride; so will you.

After returning from the ride, immediately put on your running shoes and head out for a five-mile run.

Day 7 (Sunday)   This will be the first of your long Sunday runs. The idea is to run about 40 percent of your weekly mileage. Since your mileage so far for Week 7 is around 15, including intervals and cool down, this Sunday will feature a brisk six-to-seven miler. Start out at a moderate pace and build speed throughout the run. Each mile should be faster than the one preceding it. Afterward, cool down with an easy mile-long jog, and then stretch and relax for at least 15 minutes. It's Sunday, so you've got the extra time.

Week 8

Week 8 Schedule

Monday: ride 10–15 miles, run 5 miles
Tuesday: ride 20 miles
Wednesday: run intervals
Thursday: ride 10 miles
Friday: off
Saturday: ride 20–25 miles, run 5 miles
Sunday: run 6–7 miles

Totals: ride 65-70 miles, run 22 miles

Repeat Week 7, concentrating on form and technique. No extra mileage, no extra speed.

Week 9

Week 9 Schedule

Monday: ride 10–15 miles, run 5 miles
Tuesday: ride 20 miles
Wednesday: run intervals
Thursday: ride intervals
Friday: off
Saturday: ride 20–25 miles, run 5 miles
Sunday: run 6–7 miles

Totals: ride 70 miles, run 23 miles

Repeat the Monday and Tuesday workouts from Week 8. Then on Wednesday go to your local track and add one 880 repeat with a 110 jog to your Day 3 running interval workout. Run the 880 after the first two quarter-mile repeats and try to average 95 seconds per quarter-mile repeat and then 200 seconds, or 3:20, for the half mile. Following the half mile, you should do a quarter-mile recovery jog.

A basic rule of thumb for speed work: whatever the distance of the interval, the recovery should be half that. So a one-mile repeat should be followed by a half-mile jog, a half-mile repeat by a quarter-mile jog, and so forth.

For your cycling intervals on Thursday do a 15-miler starting with a three-mile warm-up. Ride nine miles, alternating one hard mile with one easy, ending with a three-mile cool-down. All the other days' workouts should stay the same as Week 8.

Week 10
Week 10 Schedule
Monday: ride 10–15 miles, run 5 miles
Tuesday: ride 20 miles
Wednesday: run intervals
Thursday: ride intervals
Friday: off
Saturday: ride 20–25 miles, run 5 miles
Sunday: run 6–7 miles

Totals: ride 70 miles, run 23 miles

Repeat Week 9.

Week 11
Week 11 Schedule
Monday: ride 10–15 miles, run 5 miles
Tuesday: ride 20 miles
Wednesday: run intervals
Thursday: ride intervals
Friday: off
Saturday: run 3 miles, ride 18 miles, run 3 miles
Sunday: off

Totals: ride 70 miles, run 23 miles

By Week 11, you should be primed and ready to race. Now it's just a matter of fine-tuning your effort. Complete your Monday through Friday workouts exactly as Weeks 9 and 10. On Saturday you will simulate race day with a 5K run, a 30K bike ride, and another 5K run (3.1-mile run/18-mile bike/3.1-mile run). Set up a transition area at your house and make believe you're doing the race. Finding a few friends to do this with you always makes this workout a lot more fun. And if you can con the family into hanging out at your transition area on the front lawn, you'll have both someone to guard your equipment and a cheering section to keep you going. Think about your transitions ahead of time, and be fast and efficient getting in and out of your shoes and helmet. Enjoy yourself! Racing is your reward for all the training. Anticipate and savor it. Also, be aware of any squeaks or rattles on your bike, and during this week before the race, have your bike tuned and ready to go.

Week 12

Week 12 Schedule

Monday: ride 10–15 miles, run 5 miles
Tuesday: ride 20 miles
Wednesday: run intervals
Thursday: ride intervals
Friday: ride 10 miles if race is Saturday, or off if race is
    Sunday
Saturday: race, or ride 10 miles if race is Sunday
Sunday: race

Totals: ride 60 miles, run 10 miles

During the week of the race, your training should stay consistent, except that Friday should be an easy spin day if the race is Saturday. If the race is on Sunday, take Friday off and spin 10 miles or so on Saturday. Spend a few minutes the night before the race visualizing how you hope things will go. Think "smooth, easy, and relaxed." Come race day you're ready to run and ride like the wind. Good luck!

CHEKPOINT: BUILDING ABDOMINAL STRENGTH by Paul Chek

In my practice as an athletic trainer and sports massage thera-pist, I come across many situations that could be remedied with added strength and tone to the abdominal musculature. Many athletes use their abdomen as a reference point. When they're in shape it's flat, and when they're not, it's round. Well, there is more importance to this muscle group than physical appearance. A weak or poorly conditioned abdomen can lead to many prob-lems, causing slower times and poor performance in almost every sport. The athlete with less than sufficient abdominal strength will have less respiratory efficiency and often shows signs of anterior pelvic tilt. This leads to poor posture and biomechanical inefficiency. The underdeveloped, poorly condi-tioned abdomen affords much less flexion and rotary strength than is acceptable for good performance in most all athletic activities. Poor protection and lack of support of the internal organs can also lead to problems.

To ab or ab not. If you do your sit-ups consistently, you can end up with a washboard stomach like Paul Chek (right). If not, well . . . the choice is yours.

If you are a runner or cyclist who seems to lag on the hills, pick-ups, jumps, or finishing kicks, there is a very good chance that increasing your abdominal strength will improve your performance in these areas. Three 15–20 minute sessions a week, using a variety of abdominal exercises, will provide you with a more completely strengthened abdomen.

When doing abdominal exercises it is recommended that you not do standard sit-ups, which cause strain on the lower back. There are available good exercises that isolate the major areas of the abdomen and that are safe. Most gyms and health clubs have machines for strengthening the three major areas of the abdomen: the upper abdomen, lower abdomen, and obliques (sides).

A good, safe exercise for the upper abdomen is the crunch. It can be done by lying on your back with your fingers interlocked, hands behind your head, and legs up and bent. The key to protecting the lower back is to have the femur (the large bone of the upper leg) at a 90-degree angle to the torso. From this position you simply draw your upper body toward your raised legs, only high enough to completely contract the abdominal

Straight-leg crunch. Keep your shoulder blades flat on the floor and reach for your toes. Then relax and repeat. Try to do sets of 15–20 for this and each following exercise every time you do your abdominal workout.

muscles or until your shoulder blades are three to five inches off the floor. By alternating right elbow to left knee and left elbow to right knee, you can work the rotary or obliques. The lower abdomen can be strengthened in many ways. The most common way is flutter kicks and/or leg extensions. These exercises can be done by lying on your back and putting your hands flat on the floor under your bottom to support your lower back. From this

The bicycle. Done correctly, this exercise will burn Rambo's belly! Bring your right elbow to your left knee, keeping your right leg extended and off the floor as shown. Repeat movement with left elbow and right knee. The key here is keeping movement fluid and remembering to breathe. *Not recommended for beginners or people with any back problems.

Starting position for the crunch, which works the upper abdomen. Your shoulder blades are flat on the ground.

position extend your legs until straight and hold them approximately 12 inches off the floor. Flutter kicks can be done by alternate kicks ranging from six inches to 18 inches from either foot to the floor. Leg extensions are done simply by drawing both legs together toward your upper body until your heels are near your bottom and then extending both legs.

The last and most important point is always stretch these muscles after exercise. This can be done by lying on the floor in

To finish the crunch, bring elbows to knees to fully contract your abdomen. Your hips should be flexed 90 degrees to protect your lower back.

The cross crunch strengthens upper abdomen and external obliques. Right elbow goes to left knee, followed by left elbow to right knee.

the push-up position. From here push yourself up leaving your hips on the floor. Done properly, you should look like a cobra posed for attack. From here simply relax the abdomen and take a deep breath.

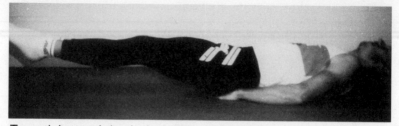

To work lower abdominals, hold your feet off the floor for a count of 10. Relax and repeat. To make the exercise easier for beginners, your feet can be as much as two feet off the ground. As you become stronger, they can go as low as six inches off the ground. Remember, *always* protect your lower back.

KEN SOUZA'S YEAR-LONG TRAINING PROGRAM

The following is my yearly training program. As you can see, I like to break up my year so that I don't burn out by the time the biathlon season rolls around. During the winter months, I try to ride my mountain bike and leave the road bike in the garage for a while. Time off makes getting back on the road new and exciting.

My background is not short-distance biathlons but long-distance triathlons. So when you look at my weekly and monthly mileage on the bike, remember that you don't need to do anywhere near that type of mileage to be competitive in a 5K run-40K bike-5K run biathlon.

My program is the result of trial and error, plus years of riding and running with the likes of Scott Molina, Scott Tinley, and Mark Allen on an almost daily basis. I've had a fair amount of success with my training, but that doesn't mean it's appropriate for everyone. Take what knowledge I offer in this book, experiment with your own training, and find what works best for you. Good luck and good training!

Winter

All my training this time of year is easy: easy running and easy gears on the bike. This is also the time of the year that I alternative train, for example, on my mountain bike.

Monday: run 6 miles, ride 20 miles
Tuesday: ride 30–40 miles
Wednesday: run 7–8 miles, ride 50 miles
Thursday: run 6 miles, ride 30 miles on a mountain bike
Friday: off
Saturday: ride 50 miles, run 6 miles
Sunday: run 7–8 easy miles

Spring

Monday: run 7–8 miles, ride 60–70 miles using big chain ring
Tuesday: run 10–12 mile fartlek, ride 30 miles using small chain ring
Wednesday: run 6 miles, ride 70–80 speed work miles
Thursday: run 7–8 miles, ride 30 easy miles
Friday: run 7–8 miles, ride 35–40 easy miles
Saturday: run 7–8 miles (or take off), ride 60–70 miles
Sunday: long, easy run for 1½–2 hours

Summer

Monday: run 7–8 miles, ride 70–80 miles
Tuesday: run 6–7 miles, ride 30–40 easy miles; run track workout (3 miles of interval training)
Wednesday: run 6–7 miles, ride 70–80 speed work miles
Thursday: run 6–8 miles, ride 30–40 miles; track workout later in the day (3 miles of interval training)
Friday: run 6–7 miles (or take off), ride 20–30 easy miles
Saturday: run 7–8 miles, ride 75 miles; or race
Sunday: run 2 hours; or race

Fall

This season involves long training, most of it at Ironman pace.

Monday: run 7–8 miles, ride 80–90 miles using big chain ring
Tuesday: run 12–14 fartlek miles, ride 50–60 easy miles
Wednesday: run 7–8 miles, ride 100 miles
Thursday: run 7–8 miles, ride 40–50 miles; run track workout (3 miles of interval training)
Friday: run 8 miles, ride 40–50 miles; or take off
Saturday: run 9 miles (or take off), ride 80 miles
Sunday: 2-hour long, easy run

BIATHLON SURVIVAL KIT
Cycling

- Bike
- Bike shoes
- Bike helmet (ANSI approved)
- Bike gloves
- Bike shorts or bike tights
- Bike jersey
- Water bottles (two)
- Pump for bike tires
- Frame pump (with gauge) for home or car
- Turbo trainer for indoor riding
- Spare tire or sew-up tire
- Tube kit (if not using sew-ups)
- Sunglasses
- Fluid replacement drink such as Exceed or Bodyfuel
- Fanny pack to carry ID, money, food, etc.

Optional:
- Aerodynamic handlebars
- Racing wheels
- Disk wheel or Tri Spokes
- Powerbar or other snack for the ride
- Money for food, drink, or emergencies on the road
- Clip-in pedal system (expensive, but worth it)
- Rearview mirror (on helmet)

Running

- Running shoes
- Shorts or tights
- Singlet
- Vaseline to prevent chafing
- Racing flats
- Sunglasses
- Socks

5
TRAINING TIPS FOR THE HARD-CORE BIATHLETE

If you've followed my basic training workouts in Chapter 4, by the conclusion of your first event your weekly mileage should be around 70 miles on the bike and 23 miles running. Before you start adding to that mileage base, let's take a look at the advancements in training that have occurred during the past few years. Gary Hooker of Leucadia, California won the 40-to-44-year-old division at the 1986 Ironman Triathlon with a time of 10:19 and also ran a 4:10 1,500 meter run at the age of 42. Hooker has been very successful training himself and others with the use of a heart monitor. He monitors his heart rate with the help of a computer that allows him to graph the results of each and every workout. This way he is very specific in his training and can be very successful with a minimal time commitment. "At all levels," he says, "given equal talent and time to train, those who are scientific and organized will always outperform the unscientific and disorganized."

Before we get into Gary's program, however, we need to define a few terms. There are three accepted measures of physiological stress: *anaerobic threshold, VO$_2$-max,* and *heart rate.*

Photo by Lois Schwartz

Running fast hurts, no matter who you are. That's why it's important to do interval training to get used to dealing with that pain. This is Arturo Barrios, one of the top road racers in the world. As you can tell, even Barrios hurts when he runs fast.

Anaerobic threshold (A.T.) is the point when lactic acid begins to accumulate in the blood. It marks the transition from primarily aerobic ("in the presence of oxygen") to anaerobic ("without oxygen") energy consumption. Lactic acid is a waste product of this anaerobic energy use. A.T. symptoms include increased muscle fatigue and soreness. It is measured in the laboratory by analyzing the blood.

VO$_2$-*max* refers to the point when oxygen use can no longer increase in spite of increased work being done. The cardiovascular system is taking in oxygen and transporting it to the muscles at maximum capacity. This point is determined in the lab by gas analysis.

Heart rate: when VO$_2$-max and anaerobic threshold tests are conducted in the lab, EKG leads are attached to the chest to measure heart rate. As the work load is increased, heart rate will also increase. When the body is using its maximum amount of oxygen (VO$_2$-max), the heart will also be operating at maximum capacity. It has been proven that there is a direct link between work load and heart rate.

The fractional heart rate pace chart that is in this chapter (see page 92) will let you match the fractional paces associated with your current performance level to your fractional heart rate (given in percentage of maximum heart rate). The chart associates the physiological points of VO$_2$-max and anaerobic threshold with ranges under the headings *maximal* and *threshold*.

By using the information in the chart and wearing a heart monitor during time trials or actual races, you can match your individual fractional heart rate to an estimated fractional pace. This information will give you the tools to construct your own training plan and evaluate your progress toward your competitive goals.

The following is a step-by-step guide to completing the fractional heart rate pace chart with an explanation of each functional level.

THE FRACTIONAL HEART RATE PACE CHART

10K	5K	10 MILE	VO2 MAX TEST (MAXIMAL) PACE	VO2 HR	1/4 MILE	95% HR	95% PACE	THRESHOLD 90% HR	90% PACE	85% HR	85% PACE	80% HR	80% PACE	75% HR	75% PACE	70% HR	70% PACE	SUB-MAX TEST PACE	%
	27:00	12:55	04:00		60		04:05		04:30		04:50		05:10		05:40		06:05	06:05	05:15
	27:30	13:10	04:05		61		04:10		04:35		04:55		05:20		05:45		06:10	06:10	05:15
	28:00	13:25	04:10		63		04:15		04:40		05:00		05:25		05:50		06:15	06:20	05:15
	28:30	13:35	04:15		64		04:20		04:45		05:05		05:30		05:55		06:25	06:20	05:15
	29:00	13:50	04:20		65		04:25		04:50		05:15		05:40		06:00		06:30	06:30	05:30
	29:30	14:05	04:25		66		04:30		04:55		05:20		05:45		06:05		06:35	06:35	05:30
	30:00	14:20	04:30		67		04:35		05:00		05:20		05:45		06:10		06:40	06:35	05:30
	30:30	14:30	04:35		68		04:40		05:00		05:25		05:50		06:15		06:45	06:45	05:30
	31:00	14:45	04:40		69		04:45		05:10		05:30		05:55		06:20		06:50	06:45	05:30
	31:30	15:00	04:45		70		04:50		05:15		05:35		06:00		06:25		06:55	06:50	05:30
	32:00	15:15	04:50		71		04:55		05:20		05:45		06:10		06:35		07:00	07:00	06:00
	32:30	15:30	04:55		72		05:00		05:25		05:50		06:15		06:40		07:05	07:05	06:00
	33:00	15:45	05:00		73		05:05		05:30		05:55		06:20		06:45		07:10	07:10	06:00
	33:30	15:55	05:00		75		05:10		05:35		06:00		06:25		06:50		07:15	07:15	07:15
	34:00	16:10	06:40	105	76	176	05:16	167	06:40	157	06:30	148	06:26	139	06:32	130	07:20	06:30	07:2?
	34:30	16:25	05:25	104	77	177	05:20	167	06:20	157	06:45	150	06:10	139	06:2?	130	07:25	06:30	07:2?
	35:00	16:40	05:30	95	78	176	05:26	167	06:20	157	06:50	148	06:10	137	06:3?	110	07:30	07:00	07:4?
	35:30	16:55	05:35	85	79	176	05:31	167	06:20	157	06:55	148	06:15	137	06:??	110	07:35	07:00	07:??
	36:00	17:10	05:40	95	80	176	05:35	167	06:30	157	07:00	148	06:25	134	06:??	130	07:40	07:00	08:2?
	36:30	17:15	05:25		81		05:35		06:05		06:30		06:55		07:20		07:45	07:45	06:30
	37:00	17:35	05:30		82		05:45		06:10		06:35		07:00		07:25		07:50	07:50	06:30
	37:30	17:50	05:35		84		05:50		06:15		06:45		07:10		07:35		08:00	08:00	07:00
	38:00	18:05	05:40		85		05:55		06:20		06:50		07:15		07:40		08:05	08:05	07:00
	38:30	18:15	05:40		86		06:00		06:25		06:55		07:20		07:45		08:10	08:10	07:00
	39:00	18:30	05:45		87		06:00		06:30		07:00		07:25		07:50		08:15	08:15	07:00
	39:30	18:45	05:50		88		06:05		06:35		07:05		07:30		07:55		08:20	08:20	07:00
	40:00	19:00	05:55		89		06:10		06:40		07:10		07:35		08:00		08:25	08:25	07:00
	40:30	19:15	06:00		90		06:15		06:45		07:15		07:40		08:05		08:30	08:30	07:30
	41:00	19:30	06:05		91		06:20		06:50		07:20		07:45		08:10		08:35	08:35	07:30
	41:30	19:45	06:10		92		06:25		06:55		07:25		07:50		08:15		08:40	08:40	07:30
	42:00	20:00	06:15		93		06:25		07:00		07:30		07:55		08:20		08:45	08:45	37:30
	42:30	20:10	06:20		94		06:30		07:05		07:35		08:00		08:25		08:50	08:50	08:00
	43:00	20:25	06:25		95		06:35		07:10		07:40		08:05		08:30		08:55	08:55	08:00
	43:30	20:40	06:30		96		06:40		07:15		07:45		08:10		08:35		09:00	09:00	08:00
	44:00	21:00	06:35		98		06:40		07:20		07:50		08:15		08:40		09:05	09:05	08:00
	44:30	21:10	06:40		100		06:45		07:25		07:55		08:20		08:45		24:45	09:10	08:00
	45:00	21:20	06:45		101		06:50		07:30		08:00		08:25		08:50		03:50	09:15	08:00
	45:30	21:35	06:50		102		06:55		07:35		08:05		08:30		08:55		09:00	09:20	08:00
	46:00	21:45	06:55		104		07:00		07:40		08:10		08:35		09:00		09:05	09:25	08:00
	46:30	22:00	07:00		105		07:05		07:45		08:15		08:40		09:10		09:10	09:30	08:00
	47:00	22:10	07:05		106		07:10		07:50		08:20		08:45		09:15		09:15	09:35	08:00
	47:30	22:25	07:10		107		07:15		07:55		08:25		08:50		09:20		09:20	09:40	08:00
	48:00	22:40	07:15		109		07:20		08:00		08:30		08:55		09:25		09:25	09:45	08:00
	48:30	22:55	07:20		110		07:20		08:05		08:35		09:00		09:30		09:30	09:50	08:00
	49:00	23:10	07:25		101		07:25		08:10		08:40		09:05		09:35		09:35	09:55	08:00
	49:30	23:25	07:30		102		07:30		08:15		08:45		09:10		06:40		06:40	10:00	08:00
	50:00	23:40	07:35		104		07:35		08:20		08:50		09:20		06:45		06:45	10:00	08:00

(Handwritten annotations appear in the shaded band, rows with 5K 34:00–36:00, labeled "75%", arrow, and "85%".)

Step 1: Select Your Performance Level

The 10K, 5K, and 10-mile columns at the left of the chart show the statistical relationship among a person's best times in three popular racing distances. It assumes he or she is properly trained for each of the events. The ideal starting point would be to record your heart rate during a race or time trial at one of these distances. If this is not possible, select your performance level based on your most realistic estimate of current times.

Step 2: Determine Your Maximal Heart Rate

You cannot effectively use heart rate in your training and racing plan until you know your maximal heart rate (max h.r.). Most athletes don't. Research has shown that 220 minus age is not an accurate estimate of max h.r. In 1987 Gary Hooker tested more than 30 elite age group athletes at the United States Cycling Federation National and California District Championships. These athletes ranged in age from 20 to 75 years. He found almost no relationship between age and max h.r. He tested a 70-year-old man with a max h.r. of 175 beats per minute (bpm) and a 24-year-old with a max h.r. of 180 bpm. In 1987, Dave Spangler, age 45, set the 40K time trial record (52:55) for the 40–45 age group; he has a max h.r. of 197. Norm Hoffman, age 46, set the 45–50 age group record (51:47) at the same race with a maximum heart rate of 167, 30 bpm less than Dave's. Obviously, 220 minus age would not have come close to calculating any of these individuals' max h.r.

Maximal heart rate is defined as the heart rate that occurs at VO_2-max. It can also be called VO_2-max heart rate, but we will simply call it max h.r. Max h.r. can be calculated in the lab during a VO_2-max test, but these tests are expensive ($250–$600). If you have taken a lab test, use the heart rate at VO_2-max as your max h.r. We will outline several ways to calculate your max h.r. using a heart-rate recorder or monitor.

Max h.r. is the most important factor to determine because all heart-rate training is based on this number. Trying a number of tests will improve the accuracy of your estimation, but once you've settled on a number, keep it. Max h.r. is genetically determined and changes little from year to year. What changes is how much work you can perform at maximum or any fractional level.

The ideal way to conduct the tests outlined below is to use a heart-rate recorder with computer-graphics capability. You can also copy the numbers from the recorder and construct your own graphs by hand. It is even possible to use a heart monitor and call out the readings to an assistant as you go.

Five-to-eight-minute test   Your heart rate during the latter part of an evenly paced time trial of five to eight minutes, or to exhaustion, is your max h.r. To perform this test, look at the performance level you selected in step one. Under VO_2-max test you will find a pace, given in both one-mile and quarter-mile splits. This is the pace at which you will conduct your test. It is important to be rested before you begin. Now the trick is to run at an even pace, so a watch that beeps at preset intervals or an assistant is helpful. Run as close as you can to the quarter-mile times. If you have selected the proper performance level, you should run four to six quarter-mile laps before exhaustion. If you cannot maintain the pace, try to finish the lap you're in and conclude the test. If you cannot run a mile at the pace listed, select a lower level and try again another day.

5K race or time trial   Your average heart rate during a 5K race or time trial will be approximately 95 percent of your max h.r. The best way to perform this test is to wear a heart-rate recorder (set to record at five-second intervals). Then graph the data, plotting heart rate vs. time. When you look at the graph, you should notice, especially in the midportion of the test, that your heart rate is seeking a certain level. Assign the proper heart rate to that level and multiply that number by 105 percent to estimate your max h.r.

10K or 10-mile time trials Your average heart rate during a 10K race or time trial will be about 93 percent of max. The procedure to follow is the same as that for the 5K trial. Multiply your average heart rate by 107 percent to get your max h.r. Similarly, a 10-mile trial is run at 90 percent of max. Multiply your average heart rate in the event by 110 percent to get your max.

When you have completed one or more of these tests and have determined your max h.r., you can arithmetically determine your fractional heart rates. To do so, multiply your max h.r. by the percentages given above each blank column and record the number in the appropriate column.

THE THREE HEART-RATE RANGES

Maximal Range
(95-110+ Percent Max H.R.)

The maximal range includes paces (work loads) that are both higher and lower than max (100 percent). For example, if an athlete's performance level on the chart indicates a 70-second quarter-mile time at max h.r., that athlete could likely do a quarter-mile race in about 58 seconds and record heart rates higher than his VO_2-max h.r. The maximal range includes an intensity above max down to 95 percent of max. Training in this range should be very limited. The training benefits are small and the risk of injury is high. We call this "no man's land."

Threshold Range (85-95 Percent Max H.R.)

Of the three ranges, threshold is the most important. Most endurance races are performed in this range, and training in this range is the only way to cause the neuromuscular adaptation required to achieve your competitive goals. Anaerobic threshold will occur within this range in most trained athletes.

Among elite athletes blood-sample tests are done at key points in the annual training cycle to chart improvements in anaerobic threshold. The higher the anaerobic-threshold percentage, the faster an athlete's competitive times should be. Our system uses the heart-rate recorder to measure improvement in pace at each fractional level. In other words, as you improve, you will run faster at the same heart rate. This should also result in faster competitive times.

As you train and race at the fractional paces listed on your performance level, your heart rates should decrease. When your competitive times improve, go to the next level, where the faster paces will again produce the desired fractional heart rates.

Base Range (70-85 Percent H.R.)

The base range is where you will do a large portion of your training. Your early season preparation, long steady efforts, and easy runs are performed in this range. Training at these levels will develop and maintain your cardiovascular efficiency and give you the base necessary to handle more intense work loads. The paces listed in this table are estimates based on heart-rate recordings.

THE SUB-MAX TEST

The sub-max test is an easy test that can be conducted frequently. It will allow you to check your performance level and measure progress within each level. The paces listed in this column are designed to produce a fractional heart rate between 75 percent and 85 percent of max. You will notice that one pace covers a wide range of performance levels. When you select a sub-max test pace, you should keep this pace from year to year. This will allow you to establish a starting point after a layoff or injury.

To conduct this test, use the same procedure as the five-to-eight-minute test. It will involve an evenly paced, one-mile run. You will record your heart rate during the last 100 yards. Take this number and divide it by your max h.r. Expressed as a percentage, this is your sub-maximal efficiency. You should record this number on a weekly or biweekly basis. It is an excellent indicator of improved performance. A large decrease in sub-maximal efficiency over a short period of time can signal overtraining.

Try some of the tests and experiment with the chart for a

few weeks. The concept should become clearer. The performance levels and fractional heart rates are also useful by themselves. Next we'll put the numbers to use in a training program.

ESTABLISH A GOAL

Figure out the level you hope to reach in training. This is your goal pace. Mark your fractional pace chart with a goal and a dateline. Your plan should be based on a training pyramid with three main phases: base, strength, and speed.

Base

Base is the foundation of your training plan. You should spend 50 percent or more of your yearly training at this level. During your base training period, you should exceed 85 percent work intensity (refer to fractional pace chart) only if you do an occasional race. After these races you should allow plenty of easy days for recovery. Training above the 85–90 percent range without proper preparation invites injury and is usually a waste of time and hard work.

The cornerstone of base training is the weekly, long, continuous effort of 70–75 percent pace. This session should make up 20–40 percent of your total weekly mileage. If you run 100 miles per week, your long run should be at least 20 miles. If you run 35 miles per week, your long run could be up to 15 miles. The long run should not be done the week of a race. Each base week should also include two quality days. These quality sessions should last about one hour and be done at 75–85 percent pace. The rest of your base-period mileage should be done at a comfortable pace, according to how you feel.

Recording your heart rates on quality days and during occasional races will give you a weekly evaluation of your progress. Slowly increase your weekly mileage and pace until you reach your goal level. This may take as little as six weeks or as long as several years, depending on your background, your goal, and your rate of progress.

If you have not made satisfactory progress during the

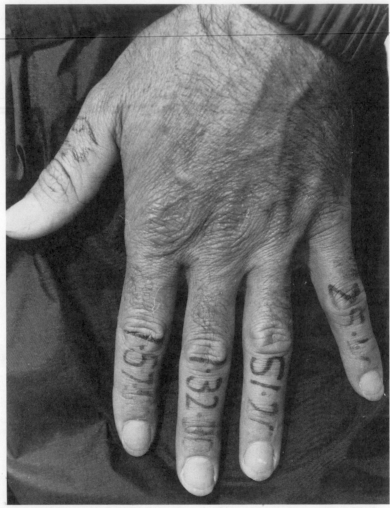

Photo by Lois Schwartz

It's good to have a plan going into any major competition. Know what you want your time to be for the first run and what you want to finish overall. The top athletes always set goals. This hand belongs to top marathoner Rod Dixon. The numbers on his fingers are the split times he planned to run at the 1988 L.A. Marathon.

period allocated for base training, for whatever reason, now is the time to change your training-and-racing plan. If you have races scheduled, either postpone them or lower your expectations. Athletes with extreme time limitations (less than eight hours per week) will probably be better off restricting their training and racing to base levels. Your body cannot successfully handle strength and speed training on an insufficient base.

It is a good idea to do a long race (two or more hours) toward the end of your base period. By recording your heart rates and pace, you can evaluate your endurance level.

Strength

The high mileage of base training should maximize your cardiovascular efficiency. Strength training begins the process of neuromuscular adaptation necessary for speed. The strength phase takes three to six weeks and develops strength and flexibility without going above your anaerobic threshold. Hill running or riding is the best way to accomplish this. Running and riding hills help to strengthen the driving muscles, the quadriceps, hamstrings, and ankles.

A typical strength-training week will have fewer total miles than your last base week. In this phase, your two quality days will be hill sessions lasting 45 minutes to one hour. You should shorten your long run about 25 percent and make it a slow recovery run. The rest of your training should be done according to how you feel, as your legs will probably be sore after the hill sessions. The multisport athlete should not do strength or speed work in more than one sport at a time.

Speed

Your base training has developed cardiovascular efficiency. You have added strength through hill work. Now you are ready for the fast stuff. Speed work is extremely stressful. To get the proper neuromuscular adaptations, you must work at speeds faster than goal pace. You must train your body to function anaerobically. Speed workouts take you beyond your capacity in a series of small extensions. Each week you go beyond the efforts of the previous week.

There are many types of speed workouts. The objective, however, is the same for each. The speed workout must build a large oxygen deficit, which creates lactic acid in the

		Run	Bike
October 4			
11	Biathlon		
18			
25			
November 1	Biathlon		
8			
15	Biathlon	Base	Base
22			
29			
December 6	Marathon		
13			
20			
27	Biathlon		
January 3			
10			
17	No races		
24	No races		Low Mileage Base
31	No races		
February 7	No races		
14			
21	10K race	34:00 10K	
28		Goal	
March 6	10K race		
13			
20			
27	Biathlon		
April 3			
10	Biathlon		
17			Base
24	Biathlon		
May 1			
8			
15		Low Mileage Base	
22			
29	USCF Regionals		
June 5			
12			
19			
26	No races		
July 3	No races		
10	No races		
17			
24	USCF Nationals	57:00 40K Goal	
31	Biathlon		
August 7			
14	No races		
21	No races		
28	No races		
September 4			
11	5K race and	15:45 5K Goal	
18	1500 meters	4:15 1500 Goal	
25			

muscles and lowers your blood pH. When you rest, your body will build buffers against fatigue, remove the lactic acid, and return the blood pH to normal. Repeating this process of stress and recovery over a period of approximately four weeks will cause your body to adapt to the higher levels of stress. Once this adaptation has occurred, it is pointless, even dangerous, to continue speed training.

Very few multisport athletes are able to take full advantage of speed training. They do not allow for proper recovery. You should not do heavy training in other sports or race during this period.

After a week or two of reduced training and sharpening, you should be ready to do your goal race. Depending on the time it took to build your pyramid, you should be able to race at your goal level for four to eight weeks. After your goal races, you can build another pyramid, starting again at base and working toward a new goal. See the chart below for examples of various training pyramids.

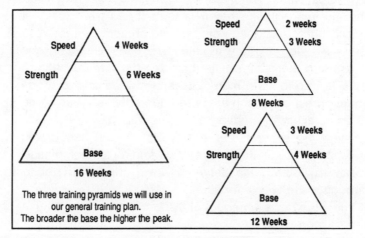

The three training pyramids we will use in our general training plan. The broader the base the higher the peak.

The chart (opposite) shows a year-long biathlon training and racing program. The goals and races are listed on the left. The training periods are listed on the right. Note that the speed portions of each sport occur at different times of the year. There are individual running and cycling goals. If you build cycling and running skills to a high level individually, these skills should carry over to faster biathlon times throughout the year. During the strength/speed phase, stay away from hard, multisport races.

CHEKPOINT: INJURIES by Paul Chek

How many of you are training right now with a physical problem of some sort? You know, a sore Achilles, sore knee, or maybe a twisted ankle. A week never goes by that someone doesn't come in and say, "This thing has been really bothering me, and it just seems to get worse." My first question, of course, is, "When did this first begin to bother you?" Very seldom is the answer less than four weeks, and believe it or not I have had athletes come in who have been training with a problem for more than a year! Keep in mind, as they say in the automotive industry, a man is only as good as his tools. Athletes can become so accustomed to the discomforts of training that when they actually begin to feel the pain associated with the onset of an acute injury, many will train through it.

Unfortunately, the next thing that happens is they begin to compensate for the problem. This puts a tremendous load on the musculoskeletal system and in turn nearly always leads to chronic injuries. The result is inability to train for an event, usually because a doctor or therapist prescribes immediate rest. I have worked with many athletes who had to be totally retrained to run with a proper, efficient stride after compensating for an injury for so long. In many cases, a strategically placed 48–72 hours of rest can mean the difference between recovering from an acute injury or creating a chronic injury!

There are several different types of pain associated with athletic training. A major key to maintaining a training base is the ability to differentiate between when and when not to train through these types of pain.

There is a certain amount of discomfort that goes with almost any training regimen. There are also several signs to back off. Exercise is a process of breaking down muscle tissue, which the body interprets as a signal to strengthen itself. The key is that if there is not adequate rest, there is a continuous breakdown, which will lead to injury *every time!*

Overtraining and sporadic training are two major causes of injury. One of the most frequently injured groups is competitive business people who travel frequently. They don't have time to maintain a routine schedule so they try to make up for lost time by compressing a week's worth of workouts into a weekend. Delayed onset of soreness is something we all deal with after that long weekend bike ride or run. This is the result of microscopic tears within the working muscles, and the pain that day (or days after) is directly related to the healing process. If there is still soreness, the healing is not complete. You should not attempt another hard effort until the pain has subsided.

Here are some definite signs that a rest period is needed:

• Reduced range of motion accompanied by pain
• Constant fatigue, often accompanied by a lack of motivation
• Lengthy warm-up required
• Nagging pains that persist
• Loss of appetite
• Increased heart rate
• Lingering muscle soreness

Anytime you have to compensate by changing your running stride or riding technique, you are definitely due for a rest period of probably no less than 72 hours from that particular discipline. The longer a rest period is delayed, the longer rehabilitation will take when your body finally gives up. Not only will you have to recover from the initial injury, but often the healthy limb begins to show signs of an overtraining injury as well as strength and flexibility imbalances. Also, you add to the retraining time it takes to obtain good form again.

The body's pain mechanism is, unfortunately, inefficient in that by the time you feel pain the damage is already in the acute stage. Any of the following signs indicate you should see a doctor, chiropractor, physical therapist, or a reputable sports massage therapist. The chances of recovering quickly will be much greater.

- Compensating for an injury
- Sharp, severe, or invasive pain
- Swelling
- Lack of performance
- Audible popping or snapping at the time of or after an injury
- Recurring pain in any one area
- Continuous referred pain (pain that is due to the injury in an area other than the injury)

The object of any athlete is to stay healthy and maintain a training base. Be aware of injuries and, more importantly, be careful not to ignore them.

6
THE RACE

Take a look at a race calendar in a national magazine such as *Triathlete* or a regional publication in your area and pick out one particular race that you would really like to do well in. Then set up a program.

Give yourself at least six to eight weeks to train sufficiently. Let's assume that the event is a sprint distance race and should take less than two hours. Keep your training the same as it has been, but start to add some more interval training to your schedule. Remember, in a short-distance biathlon the first event is a 5K run. To train to go fast in a 5K you should run quarter- and half-mile repeats during your weekly track session. Mile repeats are too long. You should be running your quarters and halves at right around race pace. It doesn't help to run sub-five-minute pace on your repeats if your goal is to run six-minute miles in the race. Run a pace that you can handle without going anaerobic.

FOUR WEEKS BEFORE THE RACE

About a month before your big race, find somewhere to test your fitness. It could be a local 10K or a time trial on the bike. If your plan is to run seven-minute miles during your 5K–30K–5K biathlon, try to average 7:10s during the 10K. If you're able to do that, you're right on target.

THREE WEEKS BEFORE THE RACE

During the last few weeks you may want to add a massage or two to help keep you loose and relaxed. If you work with one particular massage therapist, he or she can usually tell if a problem area is developing. Don't add any workouts or mileage. You're already doing all the training you need. Be confident. You're more than ready.

TWO WEEKS BEFORE THE RACE

Two weeks before the big race, find a few minutes a couple of days a week to visualize race day. See yourself staying smooth and easy during the first 5K. What will be your position? Is the terrain of the course difficult? Will it be a factor in your race?

Think about coming off the first run into the transition area. You'll put on your sunglasses, helmet, and bike shoes; mount up; clip into your pedals; and take off. Visualize banking into the turns, accelerating through the straight-aways, and staying in a gear that you can control. If the gear starts to feel too tough, shift down. Work the hills, and remind yourself to drink early and often. Gear down during the last two miles of the ride. Visualize getting out of your bike shoes, dropping your helmet, lace locking tying your running shoes, and taking off for the second run. It's amazing, but sometimes after you visualize the perfect race, on race day it almost seems like you've been there before.

THE WEEK BEFORE THE RACE

You may want to sit back and rest up during this last week, but don't—you might go stale. If you cut out any part of your training, drop your running intervals for the week

You can talk technique all you want, but sometimes you just have to put your head down and go as hard as you can for as long as you can.

and cut back on the intensity of your rides. To be safe, wear a heart monitor during your workouts to keep you from going too hard so close to race time.

Photo by Lois Schwartz

THE LAST FEW DAYS

I know some athletes who do absolutely nothing the day before a race except lie around. I know others who relax two days before and work out lightly the day before. I like to go out the day before, spin 10–15 miles, and run an easy 20 minutes just to warm up and break a sweat. What you do during the days before your big race all depends on you. I do recommend, however, that you drink a lot of water and carbo-load by eating spaghetti, bread, etc. A race demands a lot of fuel, and the last thing you need is to wake up dehydrated or suffering from low energy levels on race morning. I go so far as to keep a water bottle next to my bed to keep from getting dehydrated.

Prepare Your Equipment

A few days before the race, take your bike to your local bike shop and have them give it the once-over. Most races require your bike be inspected beforehand. If you're mechanically inclined, you can do this yourself. Starting from the tires, make sure they don't have any cracks in them and they are set up straight on the wheel. The worst thing in the world is to be racing well and then blow a tire that you knew was about to go. If you race on sew-up tires that are glued to the rim, make sure that the glue has at least 24 hours to set before you race. The last thing you want is for your tire to roll off the rim during a hard turn.

In the 1988 Coors Light Chicago Biathlon I couldn't get the chain to move into my 12-toothed cog, the hardest one on the cluster, so I had to go most of the way in my 13. I won the race and everything turned out OK, but if someone like Joel Thompson or Jeff Devlin had been in town, I might not have been so lucky. Check your gears thoroughly. Make sure your spokes are tight, lubricate your chain, test your bicycle computer, and make sure your handlebars and seat are set up correctly. Don't make any major changes right before the race. If you go to a pre-event expo at the race site, don't get carried away and purchase a brand-new pair of

This is the scene just before the start of a run-bike-run biathlon. There's no reason to be nervous at this point. Just go out there and enjoy yourself!

handlebars, seat post, or seat. Use what you've been using in training. I learned a good lesson from 1982 Ironman winner Kathleen McCartney. She trained throughout 1987 with regular handlebars, not the aerodynamic type. A few days before the 1987 Ironman she switched to a pair of aerodynamic bars. On race day she never felt comfortable on the bike and ended up having a less than happy time of it during the run. The moral of the story: have confidence in what you've been doing. If you are going to change something, do it early in your training to give your body time to adjust.

THE NIGHT BEFORE

The most important night for getting sleep is two nights prior to the race. If you do that, being too excited to sleep the night before won't leave you too sluggish on race day. I like to watch TV and stretch out a lot the night before. Then I'll use some lotion for a little self-massage and pack up all the equipment I'll need for the next day: race shoes, singlet, socks, shorts or Speedo swimsuit, sunglasses, helmet, and

Photo by Lois Schwartz

It's great to have this group *behind* you. From left to right: Mike Pigg, Walt Rider, Mark Allen, Brad Kearns, Scott Tinley, and Andrew MacNaughton at the February 1987 Desert Princess Biathlon World Championships. Unfortunately for them, Joel Thompson and I were about 30 seconds farther up the road.

race number. Before I finally doze off, I'll again visualize the race course and the competition. Then I'll put the competition out of my mind entirely and just focus on what I need to do and how I hope the race will go.

RACE DAY

I get up about three hours before the gun goes off, take a shower, eat a piece of toast or a bran muffin, and drink juice or coffee. If it's cool out, I'll put on my tights, jacket, gloves, and long-sleeve shirt. You never know what conditions will be like race day, so be prepared. If the race is a short distance from where I'm staying, I'll put my race paraphernalia in a backpack and ride to the race site. I always like to see a race course beforehand. Where is the transition area? What is the terrain like? Is there any loose sand or gravel on the roads? I took a bad fall at a race in Princeton, New Jersey, during the summer of 1988 when I slid out on some gravel taking a sharp turn. Also, riding part of the course is good for a number of reasons. One, you'll be familiar with where you are and where you have to go, which helps you be more aggressive on the bike. Two, riding a few miles early on will loosen up your legs and help you get a sweat going. If the race marshalls are around, I like to ask them what they know about the course. Usually the marshalls are top local riders who know the area like the back of their hand. Their information is always valuable.

Setting Up Your Transition Area

When I ride in after my warm-up, I'll locate the spot where I'll ride out after the run and in after the ride. Then I'll set up my transition area, putting my helmet and sunglasses on a towel. My bike shoes are already attached to the pedals to save transition time. If you don't feel comfortable making your transition like this, leave your shoes on the towel and

Photo by Debbie Douglass-Saver

Transition time: keep your time here short. This is a bike-to-run transition. Here at the Kansas City Coors Light Biathlon, I changed shoes, dropped my helmet, and got out of there.

Scott Tinley knows how important it is to always regulate his body temperature during a long race. This shot shows the two-time Ironman Triathlon champion cooling himself at the February 1988 Desert Princess Biathlon World Championships in Palm Springs.

Photo by Lois Schwartz

change into them before you mount up. Two towels are also a must—one to place your shoes, clothes, and helmet on and one to wipe off your feet if you happen to step in dirt or sand. Put your bike in an easy gear; your legs will be tired after the first run. Always make sure you know exactly where your changing area is. There's nothing worse than having the run of your life and then not being able to find your bike. Triathlete Mark Allen once rode into a transition area, racked his bike, and began putting on a pair of shoes that he thought were his own. They weren't. Try to imagine the number-one triathlete in the world trying to jam size-seven shoes on his size-10 feet. He said later that he thought his feet had swollen up during the bike ride. Needless to say, Mark lost a tremendous amount of time because he didn't plan out his transition well enough. Don't make the same mistake! Know where you are at all times.

Getting Warmed Up

Thirty minutes before the start, I'll go out and run about two miles, but this is optional. This is to get my heart rate up and to see the running course. Then I'll take off my tights and sweats, put on my race singlet and racing flats, and do some short build-up sprints. For example, if I do 100s and 200s, I'll start out easy and build up to race pace. You need to break a sweat to get yourself good and warmed up. Remember, when the gun goes off you don't want your heart rate at 43. You want it to be at least 80. The reason is simple: a biathlon start looks like a bunch of sharks at feeding time, and if you want to be there for the main course, you have to be ready to go out hard.

THE RACE

After getting your transition area set up, pumping up the tires, checking the gears, and warming up thoroughly on the bike and in the run, it's race time. I've documented my race at the Coors Light Chicago event during the summer of 1988. If you've never done a race before, this is a good sample of what you're in for. Fortunately, after losing for the first time in nearly two years to Jeff Devlin the week before in Princeton, New Jersey, I rebounded and was the first guy to the tape in Chicago.

The First Run

At the start of the Chicago race I went out strong, completing the first mile in 4:45. I wore my heart monitor throughout the race, and my heart rate was around 187–188, about 90 percent of my maximum, during that first 5K. Ninety percent was exactly where I wanted it to be. Early on there were some uphills and downhills. I used them to concentrate on my form and my stride. By the end of the first run I had put a one-minute gap on the field.

Photo by Lois Schwartz

A good example of how to keep your transitions short and sweet. First, all you need to wear on the bike is a pair of shorts, a helmet, and a pair of shades, unless it's extremely cold. Your shoes should already be connected to the pedals. When you come in after the ride, remove your feet from your shoes, grab your singlet, and head out.

The Transition

As I ran into the first transition, I had already planned out my strategy on the bike. During the last quarter mile of the run I started asking myself questions: What gear did I leave my bike in? How did I place my bike shoes and where are my helmet and sunglasses? Where did I put my bike in the rack? I've taken a more relaxed approach to transitions than in the past, and it's helped. I find that if I plan ahead, I'm much calmer. On September 11, 1988, at the Seattle Coors Light Biathlon, my run-to-bike transition was nine seconds, and my bike-to-run was six seconds. By working on the transitions you can improve your time a great deal. My average transition time used to be in the 20-to-30-second range per station. I've learned the hard way that a slow transition can mean the difference between first and second place. At the 1988 Bud Light USTS National Triathlon Championships in Hilton Head, South Carolina, Mike Pigg beat Mark Allen by 10 seconds. Their 2K swim times were about the same; Pigg went two-and-a-half minutes faster during the 40K bike ride, and Allen gained three minutes back during the run. Pigg won the national championships because his transitions were faster than Allen's.

The Ride

When I first begin my ride, my legs usually feel like logs. But that morning in Chicago, I was feeling good, moving at about 26–27 miles per hour for a while; then I accelerated to 29–30 miles per hour on the straightaways. There was gravel on some of the turns so I took it easier than I had the week before in New Jersey, when I wiped out in one of my

Photo by Lois Schwartz

If you wait until you're thirsty before you drink, you'll be dehydrated before you know it. Force yourself to drink water or replacement fluids throughout the race.

It's important to keep yourself cool on the bike, too.

Photo by Lois Schwartz

turns. I had one water bottle on the back of my bike and drank half of it during the first three miles. By 20K I had finished the rest and threw the bottle away. Coming back was tricky because I had to weave around the 1,500 people who were heading my way. I switched to an easier gear toward the end of the ride just to get my legs loosened up and ready for that second run.

The Second Transition

During the last two miles of the ride I always get a little antsy. I can't wait to get off that bike seat. Use this time to concentrate on the next transition and visualize your changing area. Before you get to the rack, unsnap your helmet, unvelcro your cycling shoes, and slip your heels out. I keep my feet in, so I'm still cycling. When you get to the rack, coast, pull your feet out, and hop off the bike. Slip your running shoes on, and when you bend over to pull the lace locks tight, let your helmet fall off. You've just completed two steps. I keep Vaseline on the outside of the heel

Photo by Lois Schwartz

Really concentrate on your form during the second run of a run-bike-run event. Top amateur biathlete Dan Rock, pictured here, recommends using your racing flats for the first run and your training shoes for the second one. He feels that because the legs are so fatigued from the first run and the ride, there is more chance for injury in your lighter, less supportive shoes. You can't argue with the guy's results. Rock is one of the most consistent biathletes around, having won his division at the Desert Princess World Championships and at the Bud Light Ontario National Championships.

counter of my running shoe in case I need to rub some between my thighs to prevent chafing. I also keep a little bit underneath my bike seat in case I need it during the bike.

The Second 5K

During my second run, I like to start out at a moderate pace unless someone like Jeff Devlin or Joel Thompson is right there with me. Then I have to go hard right off the bat. Your legs are going to feel a little rubbery at the beginning, but remember, you're using a whole different set of muscles

Under the heading "People I don't like to see at the starting line because they're too &*%$# fast" are . . .

Greg Stewart . . .

now. Ease into it. You should start to feel better after a quarter or half mile.

Coming off the bike in Chicago, I knew I had a comfortable lead. Lucky thing! I had problems getting my helmet unsnapped and eventually had to take my sunglasses off and squeeze out of it. On my way out of the transition area, I

Jay Larson . . .

made sure to ask which way to go. With a big lead and cheering spectators lining the road, all I was looking to do was maintain a smooth, strong pace. My first thought, though, was to go hard because of my loss the week before. I imagined Jeff Devlin was behind me and I had to push. Then I remembered that I had scheduled races for the next five weekends and backed off the pace.

and Joel Thompson.

At the aid station I drank one cup of water and splashed another on my head. After the turnaround, I was at the two-mile mark before the second-place guy was at mile one. So I just tried to stay light and smooth. My heart monitor read 178, 10 beats lower than during the first run. I ended up winning by about six minutes.

The moral to this story is that if you stay relaxed and race *your* race, you'll ultimately reach your goal. Sure, you could argue that my closest competitor was six minutes back so of course it was easy to stay loose. But whether you're far out in front or in the middle of a pack of fire-breathing biath-letes, your goal is to race your race, the best way you know how.

The nice thing about racing is that you can put everything on the line and try to outsprint your best buddy to the finish . . .

. . . and afterwards he's still your best buddy. If you lose to him this week, you might get him the next time around. The two guys in the photos? Top American miler Steve Scott (in the white) and the great Brazilian 800- and 1,500-meter man Joaquim Cruz.

Photo by Lois Schwartz

CHEKPOINT: USING SPORTS MASSAGE
by Paul Chek

If I were to offer you a product that could speed recovery time from exercise, reduce chance of injury, optimize your athletic potential, and still allow you to pass a drug test, would you buy it? So would I. For many years, the Europeans, especially cyclists and Russian athletes, have been the leaders in the use and research of sports massage. This, as you might imagine, contributes greatly to their strong performances in international and Olympic competition.

Here in the United States sports massage is growing rapidly in popularity. Our Olympic and professional athletes have learned the value of this from their competition and are now becoming accustomed to its benefits. Unfortunately, most of the athletes who need this service are living on a shoestring budget and cannot afford it. This means that the elite athletes who can afford it become more and more superior in performance to the sub-elite.

While working with Ken Souza to keep him racing strong and injury free, I came to the conclusion that an athlete with his training load could easily use a massage every day. When you combine two leg sports on a daily basis there is a tremendous potential for overuse injuries.

Sports massage comes in four forms: pre-event, training, postevent, and curative.

Pre-Event Massage

Pre-event massage is used to stimulate the nervous system and prepare the muscles to take on a work load. This is usually done in conjunction with stretching. Pre-event, though very effective, is the least used in its true form. When properly administered, pre-event massage will leave you feeling warm, loose, springy, and energetic. At many races, you see large groups of massage therapists doing pre-event massage. Pre-event massage requires a thorough understanding of the athlete's personality and present mood or emotional state as well as the individual's physiological response to massage. This makes pre-event massage a gamble for the athlete and the therapist who don't know each other.

Training Massage

Training massage is really the meat and potatoes of sports massage and is used most commonly one to three times a week, depending on training intensity and finances. Training, or maintenance, massage is specifically designed to keep the athlete training at a high level. Training massage is also very effective in improving circulation, removing knots and adhesions, reducing spasms, and breaking up scar tissue formation. These factors alone make it irreplaceable.

Regular training-massage sessions give the therapist a chance to maintain the athlete's flexibility and identify areas that need special attention. Your massage therapist should have a thorough knowledge of the muscle tendons used in your sport. Along with an educated sense of touch, this will enable the therapist to give you warning when injury is lurking. In the past I have been able to make several successful preinjury predictions for biathletes. The three most common areas I have been able to do this with are the origins and insertions of the hamstring muscles, the attachment of the quadriceps to the knee, and the heads of the gastrocs (large calf muscles). These areas will become painful to the touch long before they begin to give you a pain warning signal on their own. By identifying changes in the consistency of the tissues, your massage therapist should be able to tell you when to effectively back off in mileage and/or intensity. There have been several occasions when I have had to strongly suggest a reduction in training to both the amateur and the elite athlete to prevent injury and protect their training base. Unfortunately, there are those who pay for my advice but don't utilize it. They eventually come hobbling to my door with a scolded-puppy look and a dysfunctional body part.

Postevent Massage

This is probably one of the most popular forms of massage. Postevent massage is a chance for many to get a quick taste of massage, usually administered free after the races, in a shaded spot near the finish line.

Postevent is used chiefly to calm the nervous system after a hard race and improve circulation in a resting state. The other purposes are to remove catabolic (harmful to tissue) waste products, which are a by-product of energy metabolism, and identify any new injury development.

Recovery time is greatly reduced after a race that includes postevent massage. This makes it even more valuable to the athlete who chooses to race frequently and has a high-mileage training schedule.

Postevent massage should not be administered until the athlete has had a chance to cool down, drink, relax, receive his or her awards, and have a shower. The purpose for this delay is to give the nervous muscular activity and cellular metabolism a chance to slow down. Once this is accomplished, the athlete is much more ready to receive a massage, both mentally and physically.

Curative Massage

Curative massage is used specifically to treat injury. It is by far the most technical form of massage therapy and requires the most skill to administer.

There are many massage therapists who can do pre-event, training, and postevent massage but lack the training, self-confidence, and skill to do curative work. When you treat an injured athlete, you have to work with injured tissue that is very sensitive to the touch. There is a fine line between speeding up or prolonging the healing process. A therapist develops curative ability through experience.

It is my recommendation that before you seek out a good

curative massage therapist or let one attempt to help you, seek appropriate professional advice. There are many situations where massage therapy is counterproductive. A reputable registered physical therapist or sports medicine doctor is the one to give the go-ahead for a safe attempt at curative massage.

Curative massage is very effective treatment for most sport-related injuries to muscles, tendons, and ligaments; in a clinical environment, it is applicable to some joint problems.

If you need a curative massage therapist and don't know one, any elite athlete, coach, trainer, or sports-medicine clinic can usually direct you to a reputable one.

THE WELL-DRESSED BIATHLETE

From top to bottom, everything you'll ever need:

- Helmet
- Sunglasses
- Racing outfit. I like to wear just a singlet and a Speedo swimsuit. The way I figure it, the less you wear, the less you have to carry.
- Shifters at the end of the handlebars
- Bike computer
- Watch with a stopwatch function
- Bike shoes and strapless pedals. In the old days the bike pedal had a cage that you put your foot into; then you strapped your foot down. The strapless pedal is a lot less confining and a lot more comfortable. The shoe has a velcro strap for easy on-and-off.
- Brakes within easy reach
- Two water bottles, one with plain water and one with an electrolyte replacement drink like Bodyfuel or Exceed
- Disk wheel. When you ride with a disk it helps you slice right through the wind. On a hilly course with a lot of crosswinds, a disk wheel is counterproductive. But on a flat and fast 40K (25-mile) course, it can save you as much as one full minute!
- Aerodynamic handlebars. Because of the way they are designed, you can stretch out and actually place your hands in front of your face, sort of like a ski racer in a tuck. Wind-tunnel tests have proven that aerodynamic handlebars can save you at least one full minute on a flat, 25-mile bike course.

7
ALTERNATIVE TRAINING

If you do anything long enough, it gets old. This even includes fun stuff like running and cycling. When you wake up in the morning and actually dread getting on your bike, take the hint: you're burned out. Put your two-wheeled creature in the garage for a while and take a few weeks to try something a bit different. I ride occasionally with former world champion cyclist Marianne Berglund of Team Lycra. I know for a fact that when her racing season ends in November her strength coach, Ron Smith, has her put the bike away for a full month. Instead of riding, she works hard in the weight room and then plays around on her mountain bike.

No matter who you are, recharging the batteries is a necessity of life. Here are a few ways to stay fit and recharge the batteries at the same time.

WEIGHT TRAINING

I like to lift weights throughout the year. Since the bulk of the biathlon season occurs during late summer and early fall, I like to take time during the winter to concentrate on my circuit-training routine. Instead of going into the weight room twice a week like I do during the season, during the winter I'll go in three times a week. I set specific goals for my off-season workouts. For example, if I happen to be doing 10 three-quarter squats with a certain amount of weight, I'll set a goal of 10 reps with 10 percent more weight by the end of my month-long program. You'll find that weight lifting helps tremendously when you return to your power cycling workouts.

MOUNTAIN BIKING

I love my mountain bike. It gives me the ability to really get away from it all, to get out and explore. I'm amazed at what a great workout I get. Remember, a mountain bike is heavier than a road bike, usually by three or four pounds. You're going to be riding up steep, dirt-and-rock-covered trails on a heavier-than-usual bike. Mountain biking is a great strength builder.

If you go out with a group, a fun game to play is follow the leader. The leader hammers up hills, flies through rivers, jumps over small moguls. Everyone has to do the same thing. This game will help you develop bike-handling skills that definitely come in handy on the roads.

Another workout I like is ride and tie. Don't be confused by the name, which comes from a sport that makes use of two runners and one horse. One person starts out on horseback, rides a few miles before dismounting, ties the horse to the nearest tree, and heads off on the run. His partner runs up, unties the horse, mounts, and rides up the trail. The race ends when each team of three gets to the finish line.

In our ride-and-tie workouts, the horse is replaced by the mountain bike. I'll go out to a local canyon with a friend, and we'll go 12 to 15 miles trading off riding and running. Besides being a blast, it's a great workout for practicing transitions.

The key to purchasing a mountain bike, just like a road

bike, is finding a shop that will fit you correctly and understand your needs. Even if you never use one off-road, a mountain bike is still a lot of fun for tooling around town. With three sprockets on the front you can climb anything. And with a big, wide seat, thick tires, and upright handlebars, mountain bikes are both comfortable and virtually indestructible.

CROSS-COUNTRY SKIING

Of course, access to snow is your major priority here. If that's no problem, then you've got an outstanding avenue for cardiovascular fitness. Cross-country skiing is becoming a hugely popular sport, and it's getting bigger every day. In the old days cross-country skiers wore black leather low-cut boots and skis with funny bindings that looked really loose and went strolling through the woods on a pair of long planks. Sounds dull, right? Not anymore. "Skating" has changed the entire sport. Most cross-country resorts make tracks across the meadow, and the skaters fly on by.

Instead of walking straight—one foot after the other—the skater shifts his or her weight from side to side and emulates the motion that we are more used to seeing on ice or on wheels. Cross-country skiing will turn you into an aerobic animal. You'll burn 1,000 calories an hour with a heart rate higher than 150. Marathon and 10K cross-country ski races are as common in the mountains nowadays as 10K running races are in town. And the good news is that you can learn all you need to know in just a few lessons. There are even biathlon and triathlon events that involve cross-country skiing. The biggest one is the Mountain Man Triathlon in Colorado, which consists of cross-country skiing, snowshoeing, and ice skating.

SNOWSHOEING

Snowshoeing is the easiest of the winter sports for the biathlete to adapt to. Basically, you're running with gigantic shoes on your feet. The snowshoes are bulky and cumbersome, but technique is not as essential as it is in cross-country skiing. At the 1988 Mountain Man Triathlon, 1987 triathlete of the year Kirsten Hanssen made up a huge amount of ground during the snowshoe leg, primarily because the sport demands cardiovascular fitness and strength, things a fit biathlete or triathlete has in abundance. She held onto her lead during the ice-skating leg and won the event hands down.

ICE SKATING OR SPEED SKATING

This is another sport that requires a fair amount of technique. Because of the constant use of the upper leg muscles in skating, there is a significant carryover from cycling to skating. Eric Heiden became a world-class cyclist on the 7-Eleven team, making good use of the power he originally developed while winning five Olympic speed-skating gold medals.

IN-LINE SKATING

A fairly recent development in the world of fun and fitness is Rollerblades, or in-line skates. Instead of having four wheels like standard roller skates, Rollerblades use skates that look and respond a lot like hockey skates. The wheels are lined up one in back of the other, and the skater moves from side to side, just like in skating on ice or snow. The quadriceps and the muscles of the lower leg are used extensively for in-line skating.

SWIMMING

I know, the reason we all became biathletes in the first place was to avoid water and swimming. But in terms of off-season conditioning, there's nothing better than getting involved in an organized swim program in your neighborhood for a few months to build your cardiovascular fitness without pounding the pavement.

Swimming puts very little stress on the joints of the body, and if you know you don't have to swim in a race, the sport can be downright enjoyable. Again, swimming is great as a change of pace. You'll spend so much time facedown looking at the tiles on the bottom of the pool, it will make you appreciate getting back on your bike again.

SURF SKIING OR KAYAKING

This is another way to have fun, either in the ocean or in a local lake or bay. Balance and coordination are at a premium here because both the surf ski and the kayak tip very easily. I would definitely recommend lessons. The first time I took out a surf ski, I was on the verge of tipping every second. It took me a while to coordinate the steering, which is controlled by foot pedals, and the paddling, in which you use a single, double-bladed paddle.

A kayak can be used anywhere. Since you are actually wedged inside it, you need to learn how to right yourself when the kayak tips over, which it has an amazing propensity to do.

I've never tried white-water kayaking, but it looks like it would be not only one heckuva workout but also an incredibly exciting experience.

OCEAN SPORTS

No matter how much you might hate swimming, it's really hard to hate ocean sports like surfing, body surfing, or boogie boarding. Anytime you're out in the ocean, you're bound to get a great upper body workout. Paddling through the waves builds your shoulders, forearms, and abdominal muscles.

Surfing

The first thing you need here is a nice, warm wet suit. Don't leave home without it. There's nothing worse than getting cold out on your board.

Surfing is the type of sport that looks simple from the

During the off-season I like to go to my local fitness center and ride the Life Cycle. It's different, it's fun, and it's a great workout.

shore but really isn't. There are many centers on both coasts that teach surfing, and most will start you out on a large, foam surfboard for a couple of reasons. One, you don't want to find out what a fiberglass surfboard feels like on the back of your head, and two, it's very difficult to learn how to stand up on a surfboard. Your instructor invariably will start you out with a board that is very wide and easy to get up on. After buying a board, a leash (wrapped around your ankle so you won't have to swim a mile to retrieve the board every time you wipe out), a wet suit, and some sunscreen, you'll find that surfing is a pretty inexpensive sport. All you need is a few lessons on technique and reading the ocean, a few waves, and you're ready to go!

Body Surfing

Body surfing may not require as much equipment as board surfing, but technique is even more essential. The body surfer needs a pair of fins so that he or she, after picking out a wave, can swim and kick into it. When you've caught the wave, the priority is to *stay* in the wave. That means holding your breath for as long as possible, because if you lift your head up, there's a good chance the wave will continue on without you.

A major mistake a lot of rookies make has to do with direction. After you catch the wave, you want to go either left or right. If you go straight, the wave has a tendency to break over you, smashing you right into the sand.

Boogie Boarding

This is the easiest of the ocean sports to learn, and all you need is a foam board with either a single or double fin on the bottom. The rule of thumb is that the more fins there are, the more maneuverable the board is. The boogie board has a leash that is wrapped around the wrist. The boogie boarder paddles out past the breakers, using swim fins to help generate the speed necessary to get into the wave. When the wave has been selected, the boogie boarder kicks and paddles into it, then heads either right or left after the wave has been caught. As you become more accomplished, you'll find that you can do a number of exciting things on that small piece of foam.

I had a friend in high school who brought the same lunch to school every single day. A peanut-butter-and-jelly sandwich on whole wheat, a bag of potato chips, a large milk, and three Fig Newtons for dessert. I'm sure that after a while he never even tasted his meal.

The key for all of us is to stay hungry without losing our taste for what sport is all about. I'm talking variety here—variety plus excitement and adventure. I've included just a sampling of some of my favorite out-of-sport activities. There are, of course, thousands more. Don't eat the same meal of running and cycling every single day. Not only will alternative training help you mentally, but I guarantee that it will also help your cycling and running.

CHEKPOINT: THE BIATHLON TROUBLE SHOOTER'S GUIDE by Paul Chek

With a lifelong background in competitive athletics, plus my experience as a therapist, I have seen many injury patterns emerge. This trouble-shooting guide is a summation of the most common causes for the problem areas listed. The best way to utilize this information is to look at the probable causes listed under your problem area. Go through the probable causes one at a time and then determine what you have or have not done.

For example, if you have neck pain look under that heading. If you stretch regularly, then move on to the next probable cause. If you ride your bike with a military combat helmet, your head will be safe but you might want to build your neck up to handle the weight or buy a lighter helmet!

As you narrow down the list of causes, you might find such reasons as muscle strength imbalance left. If you've covered all other bases, then I recommend you see a sports medicine professional who can evaluate your strength and flexibility as well as the many other probable causes not listed.

The importance of not training through pain cannot be emphasized enough. If you ignore the pain, your body will begin to compensate immediately by developing patterns that are inefficient and very hard to break.

Toe Pain

1. Poor-fitting running or biking shoes
2. Too tightly laced running or biking shoes
3. Callus development during training
4. Worn-out running shoes
5. Running too much on uneven terrain
6. Referred or secondary pain from ankle

Heel Pain

1. Worn-out running shoes
2. Poor-fitting heel in running or biking shoes
3. Improper shoe types for your biomechanics
4. Referred or secondary pain from calves or ankles

Ankle Pain

1. Improper rehabilitation of past injury
2. Sprained ligament from twisted ankle
3. Torque in ankle from improper cleat adjustment
4. Worn or improper running shoes
5. Tendon strain at medial or lateral ankle joint
6. Lack of stretching of associated muscles

Knee Pain

1. Improper pedal adjustment
2. Improper seat height
3. Worn or improper running shoes
4. Unrealistic work/rest ratio when doing speed or hills
5. Incomplete rehabilitation of past injury
6. Lack of stretching of associated muscles
7. Secondary or referred pain from thigh problem

Thigh Pain (Quads, Hamstrings, Adductors, Glutes)

1. Improper seat height and/or position
2. Compensation for another problem area
3. Too much downhill running
4. Unrealistic work/rest ratio
5. Lack of stretching
6. Leg length discrepancy
7. Pelvic misalignment
8. Secondary or referred pain from low-back problem
9. Incomplete recovery from past injury
10. Bursitis development under iliotibial band at hip
11. Muscle strength imbalance

Low-Back Pain

1. Handlebar stem too long
2. Seat too low
3. Top tube too long—change goose neck
4. Inadequate break-in of aerodynamic handlebars
5. Compensation for weak hip extendors
6. Downhill running
7. Leg length discrepancy
8. Rotated pelvic problem
9. Muscle strength imbalance
10. Lack of flexibility or stretching
11. Worn-out running shoes
12. Reaction to gluteus and/or hamstring stress
13. Poor postural habits
14. Inadequate rehabilitation of past injury

Abdominal Pain

1. Secondary or referred pain from groin
2. Excessive abdominal exercise
3. Compensation for thigh or back injury
4. Too much hill running
5. Using too big a gear climbing a hill, resulting in excessive upper body usage
6. Food or fuel replacement that is causing gas

Neck and Shoulder Pain

1. Lack of stretching or flexibility
2. Muscle strength imbalance
3. Running too stiff in upper body
4. Residual stress from cross-training with other sports, specifically swimming
5. Helmet too heavy or neck too weak
6. Gooseneck and/or top tube too long
7. Inadequate break-in of aerodynamic handlebars

8. Excessive arm swing while running
9. Uptight posture when cycling
10. Incomplete rehabilitation of past injury
11. Work- or family-related emotional stress
12. Compensation for low-back or leg pain, specifically while running
13. Kinked neck from unusual sleeping position
14. Worn-out running shoes
15. Overuse of weight training

Wrist and Hand Pain (or Tingling, Numbness)

1. Top tube or gooseneck too long
2. Worn-out cycling gloves
3. Holding one position for too long
4. Secondary or referred pain from neck and shoulder problems
5. Too tight or fearful grip on handlebars
6. Cycling gloves too tight
7. Riding rough pavement, cobblestones, etc.
8. Incomplete rehabilitation of past injury
9. Weight training or work stress showing up on the bike

8
BIATHLONS AROUND THE COUNTRY: THE BIGGEST, THE BEST, AND A FEW OF THE REST

There's no doubt the sport of biathlon is growing; biathlons are where triathlons once were, poised at the edge of a boom. Many people believe that the biathlon will eventually outstrip the triathlon, and after looking at a few simple facts, this isn't hard to imagine. There are an estimated six million competitive runners in the United States and some 20 million people who ride a bicycle for exercise—not just around the block to drop off a letter but specifically for exercise. That's a lot of runners and cyclists, and it doesn't take a genius to see that the biathlon caters to their tastes.

Probably the biggest boon to biathlon, though, is what it doesn't have—a swim. Swimming has never been my strong suit, and I don't think I'm wrong in saying I'm not alone. Those involved in biathlons point to the untold millions of potential multisport athletes who are looking for a challenge but haven't taken up the triathlon because of the swim. But they're out there, and they're looking.

If you don't believe it, just ask Joe Kratovil. Kratovil hosts a race in Princeton, New Jersey, called the Princeton Forrestal Village Biathlon. The Princeton race grew out of several

139

smaller biathlons, and Kratovil has never had a problem filling his races. However, even he received a jolt when the *New York Times* ran a brief article on biathlons a month before his 1988 race. As a direct result of that article, Kratovil received more than 250 phone calls from wanna-be biathletes—people who had never even heard of biathlons but thought they sounded interesting. Kratovil, a generally unflappable man, admits he was floored.

Because of the sheer numbers involved, it's impossible to list a representative sampling of biathlons, which stretch from Saskatchewan, Canada, to Panama City, Florida. What I've done here is list a few of my favorites along with a smattering of unique biathlons that may pique your interest and get you involved in the sport. As you can see from even this short listing, there is a race out there for everyone—from short dashes to races that will bring you to your knees and truly test your mettle. If you don't see anything

The Desert Princess Biathlon World Championships, one of the most beautiful race courses anywhere.

Photo by Lois Schwartz

Photo by Lois Schwartz

At the Desert Princess Biathlon event, the first 10K seems fairly easy. After a 40-mile ride, though, the second 10K on loose dirt and sand can seem like forever. I've learned my lesson the hard way. I don't play hero anymore during that first 10K; I just run with the group.

here that stokes the competitive fires, maybe you should sell your bike and invest in a recliner.

The Desert Princess Run-Bike-Run
Palm Springs, California

Ouch. What more can you say about a race that drags you through 50 miles of desert and pits you against bone-dry heat and brutal head winds? On paper the Desert Princess 10K run/62K bike/10K run doesn't appear to be all that demanding, but ask anyone who's done the race and you'll receive a more accurate appraisal. Joel Thompson, one of the best biathletes in the business, calls the Desert Princess brutal, and I don't think there are too many people (including me) who would disagree.

It's funny, but even when you see the course it doesn't appear to be that challenging. Sure, it loops through the desert in and around Palm Springs, one of the driest places you're likely to encounter, but the course appears relatively flat. This isn't exactly true; the bike course is littered with inclines so gradual that at first glance they are virtually invisible—until you're on a bike, plowing up them and wondering when they're going to end.

Then there's the run—again flat, and again just about as grueling as they come. Both 10K runs are on the same course; first you loop around the Desert Princess Resort on nice, firm pavement, then you head out into dirt and scrub. The first 10K run isn't bad unless you're chasing Mark Allen. But by the time you dismount for the second run, that once-flat course seems to have transformed itself into something else altogether.

There's no doubt the Desert Princess race offers a challenge, and that challenge has drawn some of the best names in the business—Mark Allen, Mike Pigg, Scott Molina, Scott Tinley—who, not surprisingly, have provided me with some of my biggest challenges. Race directors Greg Klein and Brenda Clark held the first race in November 1986, and since that time their three-race series (one race in November, one in January, and one in February) has become one of the premier events on the circuit.

Before you write this one off as too difficult, realize that the Desert Princess series also features a 3K–15K–3K "Fun 'N Sprint" course that is more popular than Levi jeans in Russia; at the February 1988 event, 420 people competed in the short-course race, and Greg and Brenda had to turn another 150 away. The February event was also billed as the world championships, and though you can call an event whatever you want, Greg and Brenda backed their claim by putting up $10,000 in prize money and assembling one of the hottest fields of competitors ever. Though I don't particularly enjoy being chased by the likes of Mark Allen, Mike Pigg, Scott Tinley, Greg Stewart, and Brad Kearns, I do appreciate what the Desert Princess has done for the sport.

The New York Biathlon Series
New York, New York

Here's your chance to see New York's five boroughs without springing for cab fare. The New York Biathlon Series features five biathlons: one each in the Bronx, Queens, Staten Island, Brooklyn, and Manhattan. Each race is a 3-mile run/20-mile bike/3-mile run—what race director Daniel Honig calls the 10K format of biathlons.

Honig, who serves as president of New York's 1,500-member Big Apple Triathlon Club, thought biathlons and America's biggest apple were a natural combination, and time has proved him to be correct. Starting with the country's largest metropolis in his pocket, Honig, the consummate promoter, has spread the word up and down the East Coast, attracting plenty of out-of-towners. The New York Biathlon Series has become a tremendous success.

The series opens with an April race in the Bronx, then bulldozes its way through spring, summer, and fall with races in May, July, October, and November. The big event of the season is the November closer, a biathlon held in Central Park. If the locale isn't enough to add wings to your feet, the competition surely will; the race is designated by the U.S. Biathlon Federation as the National Biathlon Championship. You can't sign up for this one—you have to earn your way by qualifying through one of the New York series races or some 20 other designated qualifiers scattered around the world. It's still a big field, 500 participants in all, but it contains many of the top age groupers along with many of the best pros. Mark Allen won the event in 1986; then I took three minutes off his course record to win it in 1987. Liz Downing, biathlon's wonder woman (see Index), won the women's event in 1987.

Honig sees a bright future for biathlon. All the sport needs, he says, is more exposure. Hoping to grab that exposure, Honig has outlined a national biathlon series for 1989 and is negotiating with television stations to film some

Photo courtesy of Bud Light USTS

Mark Allen (left), Harold Robinson (center), and Mike Pigg (right), immediately after the 1988 Bud Light USTS National Championships in Hilton Head, South Carolina. Allen ran three minutes faster than Pigg in the final 10K and finished only 10 seconds down.

of the New York races. Honig contends that once people get a glimpse of the sport, they'll flip for it. "It's not like the Ironman," he says. "You wouldn't have people saying, 'Well, that's an event I can't do.' They'll be saying, 'Why aren't I doing this event?' "

Coors Light Biathlon Series

Thanks to Coors Light and Rodale Press, in 1988 biathlon got national exposure from the Coors Light Biathlon Series. Coors's involvement, along with backing from Rodale Press (publishers of *Runner's World* and *Bicycling* magazines), represents a major coup for the sport. With 12 races scattered across the country in 1988, the series gave the biathlon the boost it needed.

Coors's rationale for picking up the biathlon was simple: no one else had done it and biathlon was an explosion waiting to happen. So program organizers settled on a standard 5K–30K–5K format and then put on races in Kansas City, Denver, Houston, Seattle, Minneapolis, Chicago, Boston, Atlanta, Tampa, San Diego, Phoenix, and Brea, California. The events proved to be quite a success, drawing an average of 700 entrants per event. The September 12 race in Chicago drew 1,500, and organizers had to close the field, something I think we'll see more of in the future.

Most exciting to me is not so much the numbers themselves but what they represent. According to Anna Noel, who helped coordinate the series, at least 40 percent of the field at each of the races were first timers, which made for some pretty funny questions. "I had people calling me up and asking me if they needed to bring a lock for their bike and asking what they should wear," says Noel. They may be

Joel Thompson, winner of three of the Coors Light Biathlon Series events in 1988.

Photo by Al Zacharka/Kinematic Photography

Liz Downing in 1988 winning the Princeton Forrestal Village Biathlon, held every year in New Jersey.

naive, but these newcomers represent the backbone of the sport.

Fueled by their success, Coors hopes to expand the event to 15 cities in 1989 and maybe throw in some prize money for those of us trying to make a living at this. Prize money or no, the Coors Light Series is a major step in biathlon's evolution.

The Princeton Forrestal Village Biathlon
Princeton, New Jersey

Like most biathlons, this one began as a small, hometown affair. In this case the hometown was Morris Township, New Jersey, and the affair was the 1986 Great Swamp Biathlon. It was, admits race producer Joe Kratovil, "a very small and very low-key event" with 250 athletes competing for nothing more than the sheer fun of it.

Kratovil originally began putting on triathlons for the folks in northern New Jersey, but he quickly recognized biathlon's potential when the biathlons he hosted filled to

Photo courtesy of Kinematic Photography/Al Zacharka

The guy in front of me here at the Princeton Forrestal Village Biathlon is Jeff Devlin, the eventual winner. His best 10K time? 30:02!

capacity. Excited by the prospect of this new and burgeoning sport, Kratovil lured some pros to his Great Swamp race in 1987. The race got some footage on ESPN and by the time Kratovil got around to organizing the 1988 event, the Great Swamp Biathlon had outgrown Morris Township. Kratovil shopped around for a new locale, settling on Princeton's Forrestal Village—a picturesque town within a town modeled after a European village, complete with narrow, winding streets and circles dotted with water fountains.

Kratovil then assembled a field thick in talent, with 50 pros from across the country, and pitted them against each other over a 3-mile run/20-mile bike/3-mile run. The course—two loops on the run and four loops on the cycling—was designed with spectators in mind; this is probably one of the few chances the ever-loyal support crew gets to see favorite stars race. Kratovil also spiced up the action by throwing in a few premiums—prize money given to the overall leader at certain points in the race. There's no doubt that this provides a snappy incentive to the top racers; just ask Connecticut's L. J. Briggs, who somehow ran away from a lead pack moving at a 4:45 mile pace to win $250 at the end of the first run. As Kratovil puts it, premiums "kind of change everyone's thinking a little bit."

The 1988 Forrestal Village race filled a field of 550, turning away hundreds of others. Kratovil has even bigger plans for the future, plans he hopes won't leave so many biathletes out in the cold. Forrestal Village is a unique and exciting venue, and Kratovil, like many other race directors, has settled on a 3-mile/20-mile/3-mile format that seems to appeal to everyone. "Long enough to provide a challenge, but short enough so it doesn't leave people out," he says. Just make sure you sign up in time.

The Texas Cyruthon Series

Looking for a name that would stick, race director J. George Isom dubbed his 1987 three-race series the Cyruthon. Isom draws the name from a smattering of Greek, Latin, and old English—*cy* comes from cycle, *ru* comes from run, and *thon* means contest.

The Lone Star state may have been home to some of the first biathlons ever. Olympic cyclist John Howard recalls the local Austin running and cycling clubs getting together as early as 1977 to put on informal run-bike events, which in those days had predictable results. "The runners would do well in the running portion, and the cyclists would do well in the cycling portion," laughs Howard. "Nobody cross-trained back then."

Isom, a Houston-based fitness promoter, started up the Cyruthon series in 1987, holding 5K–30K–5K races in Clear Lake, San Antonio, and Houston. The June 7 race in Houston was billed as the national championships and provided quite a field. When the smoke settled, I had grabbed a 36-second victory over John Zuilhof, a biathlete from Katy, Texas, and Jan Ripple had bested 1986 Ironman winner Paula Newby-Fraser by a scant 29 seconds. The race also provided a neat twist by having us make our transition in the Houston Astrodome arena, which was a unique experience.

Isom's Cyruthon series took a hiatus in 1988, when Isom was forced to concentrate on other commitments, but Isom hopes to start up the series again in 1989. In the interim, the Coors Light Houston event stepped in neatly to fill the needs of Texas biathletes, an insatiable bunch to say the least. When Isom returns in 1989, he vows to expand the series to include some longer events, possibly even an ultra-distance biathlon. Will the biathlon have its own Ironman? Could be interesting.

The Ontario Biathlon
Ontario, California

At first glance, it seems a strange place for an event. Ontario, California, is an industrial no-man's land plopped down between Pomona and Riverside—one of those places where heavy industry labors in sooty belches. Even race director Rob Hogan admits, "It's not the most scenic of courses."

Look a little closer, though, and you'll see a locale perfectly suited to the biathlon: wide, empty roads that are, for the most part, flat and very, very fast. I have to admit I have a soft spot for the Ontario Biathlon because it's only a few miles from where I grew up. But there are plenty of other attractions.

One of the biggest is the race format. Most biathlons have gone to the run-bike-run format because it's easier to put on. In biathlon's early days, race directors found that bike-runs and run-bikes presented some logistical problems. If you put on a bike-run, you found yourself with 500 cyclists, many of them novices, adjusting their toe clips and careening about like pinballs as they tottered off after the starting gun. Then there was the problem of drafting; how do you prevent drafting when you have a pack of 400 cyclists (discounting the 100 downed at the starting line, still lashed into their toe clips) riding down the road together?

You don't. Run-bikes, while offering neat and clean starts, can often have chaotic finishes; cyclists, unlike runners, finish at speeds of up to 30 miles an hour.

Despite the logistical headaches, Rob Hogan decided that the Ontario Biathlon would be a run-bike, with five miles of running and 20 miles of biking. "It gives you the chance to go out pretty hard on the run and then just go 100 percent on the bike—not have to save anything for anything," says Hogan.

The appeal was obvious, and since its inception in 1987 the Ontario Biathlon has been a tremendous success. The 1988 race, billed as the U.S. National Championships, attracted 850 participants, which Hogan reckons was the biggest biathlon field to date. Not everyone may have been attracted just by the lure of sport, however. Hogan drummed up an arm's-length list of sponsors and raffled off some $13,000 worth of products from Timex watches to disk wheels. "I know when I go to a race I never win anything," says Hogan, who estimates that 15 percent of the folks at the 1988 race can't make that claim. It's a nice touch to a very people-oriented race.

The West Coast Biathlon Series
Venice Beach, California

Race director Bruce Mitchell claims his series was one of the forerunners of the run-bike-run biathlon format. The West Coast Biathlon Series debuted in December 1986 with the Venice Beach Christmas Biathlon, and almost 600 competitors pounded and spun through the streets of this eclectic southern California beach town on the outskirts of Los Angeles.

For that first race, Mitchell settled on a 5K–30K–5K race because he was limited for space in the cramped environs of Venice. However, Mitchell's selection of what has now become the sport's standard distance was not entirely coincidence. "I figured a 10K run was a good total and the bike should be three times as long as the run," says Mitchell. "It seemed to be a pretty good ratio." The run-bike-run format, says Mitchell, is also fairer. "A heavy-duty cyclist may be able to hang on for the first run, but that second run evens things out."

After the success of the Christmas Biathlon, Mitchell went on to host biathlons in October and December 1987, then followed up with a spring event in February 1988, which attracted 500 participants. Mitchell admits his races are low key, but hype or no, not too many people balk at the opportunity to race along the southern California coast-line. Sponsorship, however, has been a problem. Mitchell has seen two races fold because of a lack of sponsorship, and he has hosted others, he says, "strictly for the love of it."

The Tuxedo Brothers Biathlon
Indianapolis, Indiana

Indianapolis may not seem like a hotbed for biathlons, but when Don Carr and copartner Steve Locke started their Tuxedo Brothers Biathlon in 1985, there weren't too many other biathlons around. The 1985 race was held in No-vember, but Carr, Locke, and their handful of competitors found the weather to be too cool, so the race was moved to October. The first years were low-key affairs, despite the fancy name and the fact that Carr and Locke showed up in, you guessed it, tuxedos.

Times have changed, though the dress code hasn't. The 1987 Tuxedo Brothers Biathlon drew 400 competitors. Carr attributes the race's success to a 5K–35K–5K format that is within everybody's capabilities. The event also comes on the coattails of the Indianapolis Bud Light Triathlon, held at the same place three months earlier. Carr also directs the triathlon, and he takes advantage of his position. "When we send out the results for the triathlon, we throw in an entry blank to the biathlon and tell everybody to be there for that event too."

The Bi-Icycle
Saskatchewan, Canada

I threw this one in for those of you looking for a little something out of the ordinary. Five hours' driving time from Calgary, six hours from Edmonton, and nine hours from Winnipeg, Saskatchewan, Canada, is home to some pretty avid triathletes. Don Gallo, who directs the Bi-Icycle, is frank about the motivation behind his event; the September Bi-Icycle and a similar biathlon in the spring are put on to get people who are mainly involved in triathlons.

Still, the Bi-Icycle is not without its attractions. Take the format, a 7K run followed by a 33K bike. Odd distances? Gallo chose these distances intentionally to ensure the race is the pressure-free event it was intended to be. "You can't compare it to anything, so a guy has no idea what his splits are," says Gallo. Part of the race also runs along the scenic Saskatchewan River. If that isn't enough, there are even a few surprises.

"People always think of Saskatchewan as being flat," says Gallo. "Well, we've got a couple of bumps in the course that make it somewhat interesting."

CHEKPOINT: STRENGTHENING FOR THE BIATHLON by Paul Chek

As a therapist and trainer for many athletes, from kick boxers and frisbee throwers to biathletes and triathletes, I know there is no recipe for weight training that works for everyone. Any strength-training program should be personally tailored to that individual's needs because each athlete has individual strengths and weaknesses.

Biathletes get very little upper-body strength work with their daily training, so supplementary exercise should be added. This can be done in a variety of ways. Nautilus, Polaris, and Hydro Fitness are just a few of the many types of weight-training machines available. Most clubs that have these machines also have free weights. Proper coaching, I feel, makes the machines much more productive and safe. A good, general program of upper-body circuit training should be done at one to three sets on each machine three times a week. This will build upper-body strength providing the resistance is increased periodically. Most biathletes want to get stronger without gaining weight. If this is the case, I suggest using sets of 20 reps or more. This is conducive to strength and endurance training, not power development.

Because the quadriceps, calves, and iliopsoas are all prime movers in the run as well as in the bike, these are the muscles you want to make stronger if you want to go faster. These are the muscles to work in the gym, and there are a variety of machines to work with.

Elite biathletes have very strong prime-mover muscles. As you begin to get more serious as a biathlete and put in more and more mileage on the road, bigger gears, intervals, speed work, and hills will become part of your weekly schedule. The longer you train and the more competitive you are, the more your focus turns toward doing things to stay injury free. Balance in strength is a major factor in dodging injury.

A simple way to see how balanced you are without any expensive isometric testing equipment is to list the following muscles on a sheet of paper left to right: quadriceps, hamstrings (hip extendors and knee flexors), adductors (inner thigh), abductors (outer hip), calves (rotory torso, and trunk rotation). Once you do this, go to a well-equipped gym. Use Nautilus or Polaris equipment, which offers versatility of muscle group selection, safety of operation, and availability. Most clubs have instructors to help with any questions on the machines. Start by getting properly warmed up. Ride a stationary bike or skip rope—anything to work up a good sweat. Then begin by warming each individual muscle group on the list with a set of 20 reps of approximately half your estimated maximum. The muscle groups can be compared for balance.

Always start with the large muscles first. For instance, begin with the quads. Set the knee extension machine with your perceived maximum. Once you have found your maximum weight, set the machine for half that amount. Try this with the right leg and then the left. I bet one of your legs can't do it! Then lower the weight and try again with the weak leg. Do this until you get your maximum weight for each quad. Go through all the major muscle groups, keeping track of left vs. right. Anything more than a 10 percent difference is reason for strength work with the weak muscle group. Ideally, the hamstring weight setting should be 60 percent of the quadricep. But build up to it. Never rush things when you're looking to build strength.

This is far from a professionally administered isometric evaluation, but without spending any money it will give you plenty to work on. The purpose of this program is to do something that will help keep the chance of injury down. I believe, based on what I see in the clinic, that being balanced in strength and flexibility contributes greatly to your performance. Hammering your quads and calves so you can push big gears is fine for the short term, but remember that every muscle has an opposing muscle group that is much more susceptible to injury if the strength balance gets out of hand.

9
BIATHLETES ARE PEOPLE TOO

The great thing about the sport of biathlon is that anyone can be a biathlete. Any age, any size, any background—it doesn't matter. The only requirement is an interest in getting fit and maybe, just maybe, getting fast. In your biathlon training you might meet a 50-year-old mom, a 24-year-old graduate student, a 40-year-old doctor, or a 70-year-old retiree. Because biathlon demands little more than a few hours a week of running and riding a bicycle, the sport has attracted a large cross section of participants. As you will soon find out, there is nothing better than riding or running with your husband or wife, or a few buddies from the neighborhood. While the sport is definitely designed for physical fitness, the social side of group workouts should never be ignored.

Speaking of a few buddies from the neighborhood, you are about to meet some people who are already heavily involved in the sport of biathlon. Some are former triathletes who found that swimming just didn't fit into their schedules anymore. Others are biathletes-come-lately who enjoy the benefit of cross-training and have incorporated biathlon into their lifestyle.

The profiles that make up this chapter include biathletes from all over the country and from every occupation imaginable. You'll probably recognize a few of the names and faces, but for the most part these are everyday folks, just like you, who were out there in fitnessland looking for a new challenge, a sport they could call their own.

That sport is biathlon—fitness, competition, and camaraderie wrapped up in one, nice two-sport package.

Kathy and Mark Santas
Hackettstown, New Jersey
Ages 33 and 37, respectively

Kathy Santas and her husband, Mark, took up the biathlon because they were both looking for something more. Co-owners of a fitness club in Hackettstown, New Jersey, the two lifted weights and dabbled with skiing and tennis. They had never run competitively and their biking was limited to once or twice a week. Looking for a new challenge, they went out and bought new bicycles and dove right in; Kathy finished first in her age group at the Milford-Holland Biathlon, the first biathlon she entered. "All hills," she groans. "It was incredible."

The two train together in the afternoons when business at their fitness club slacks off, slipping out the door and returning in time to oversee the busy evenings. Mondays, Wednesdays, and Fridays are set aside for run training—a six-mile run on Monday, an eight-miler Wednesday, and intervals at the track on Friday. Tuesdays and Thursdays are for long bike rides, 20 to 30 miles depending on how much time they have. The Santases also set aside one weekend day for a bike ride, then take the other day off entirely. Firm believers in weight training (and with facilities at their disposal), both Kathy and Mark also lift three days a week.

There are, says Kathy, no disadvantages to having a spouse as a training partner. In fact, it may have brought

Photo courtesy of Mark and Kathy Santas

Mark Santas and Kathy Santas.

them closer together. "If one of us has a really good run, both of us feel good about it," says Kathy. "I think in a lot of couples, when there's only one person training, the other person is jealous of their time away."

There may be one problem. Since taking up the sport, Kathy has picked up more than her share of awards, while Mark has come home empty-handed. Competition in the men's divisions is simply far more fierce, says Kathy diplomatically. Mark's response to his wife's collection of trophies? "I'm scratching out her name and putting my name on them."

Their advice to first timers is to go easy; you've got nothing but time. "Put yourself on a training schedule and stick with it, but don't overtrain. In the beginning, we found ourselves overdoing it during training, almost burning ourselves out before the race," says Kathy, who along with Mark takes a day or two off before each race just to relax.

"That way we're really hungry for the race," she says. "I really get psyched up for these things."

Bill Pape.

Photo courtesy of Bill Pape

Bill Pape
Highland Park, New Jersey
Age 41

Bill Pape is somewhat unconventional in his approach. A probation officer for Middlesex County, New Jersey, and single father of two daughters, Pape is a dedicated biathlete forced to adopt a training regimen he calls "mix and match." Pape, whose job often requires house calls, will gauge the distance and if time and distance merit will turn them into workouts. A home visit 30 miles away? Pape, dress clothes and all, may make the trip by bike. The only secret is learning how to arrive looking relatively cool and crisp. "I'll wear pants that don't show being mussed," says Pape.

Pape came to the biathlon from a running background. A onetime Boy Scout "who was always last on the hikes because I couldn't keep up," Pape took up cross-country in high school and for the most part has continued to run ever since. In 1978 he bought a bike and began dabbling in bike racing but found he was never as successful as he wanted to be; although strong over the long haul, he wasn't much of a strategist. Not surprisingly, he picked up the triathlon but again found himself laboring against an Achilles heel. "I've always felt like a fish out of water," says Pape, who constantly found himself playing catch-up during the bike and run.

Then in 1984, as the sun set on another triathlon season, Pape entered a biathlon in Franklin Township. He won. The field, says Pape, was small and the leader took a wrong turn, but Pape admits he was still "really knocked out."

Pape has since established himself as a top masters (over 40) contender and an overall threat as well, despite a training schedule he admits is hit or miss. Pape attributes much of his success to a "strain but don't break" philosophy. He has, he says, learned to take training and racing in stride, pushing himself when the opportunity arises but not chastising himself for missed workouts or poor performances brought on by too little training. Though Pape has been known to call in sick to sandwich in a distance day, he can also miss a workout and give it no thought. Too often, says Pape, athletes who miss a workout or two quickly get caught in a descending spiral, easing off or stopping altogether because their training hasn't met their standards.

Along with adopting a flexible approach to training and racing, Pape offers one other sensible tip to first-time biathletes. Lay a running and biking base, then throw yourself headfirst into the fray.

"Run with runners and bike with bikers," says Pape. "That way you'll get the feeling for what it's like to bike and run fast."

Laura Lowe
Bakersfield, California
Age 27

With 15 years of running experience behind her, Laura Lowe says she had little trouble picking up cycling. "It just seemed to be almost an extension of running, but instead of standing and pushing, I was sitting and pushing," says Lowe.

Before the biathlon entered the scene, Lowe, like many other single-sport athletes looking for a breath of fresh air, threw herself into the triathlon. And like many other budding triathletes, she faced an intimidating obstacle: the swim. Then came the biathlon. At last, sighs Lowe, "a sport for us landlubbers who don't appreciate getting our hair wet."

Combining her strong running background with a natural aptitude for cycling, Lowe stepped neatly into the biathlon niche. Amateur women's champion at the highly competitive 1988 Desert Princess Biathlon Series in Palm Springs, California, Lowe also notched a series of top-five finishes at the 1988 Coors Light Series. Lowe is not particularly surprised by her success; a competent cyclist and runner, she has simply combined these abilities in a one-plus-one-equals-three format.

"It's easier to excel in the biathlon," says the self-effacing Lowe. "You can display mediocrity in both of the sports and still do very, very well."

Hoping to make the biathlon a career, Lowe runs, bikes, and swims seven days a week, interspersing workouts with a part-time job with her sponsor, Bicycle Warehouse. Although she rarely takes a day off (calling light days "days off"), Lowe offers a word of caution to the recreational biathlete.

"Don't get overly enthusiastic your first year," says Lowe, who has seen friends pick up the sport with gusto only to drop it a year later, burned out and disillusioned.

Lowe points out that this overzealous approach can also

Laura Lowe.

Photo courtesy of Laura Lowe

put a dent in your bank account. "Don't throw out that Schwinn Varsity that you bought in 1975 because all of a sudden you have to have the latest titanium frame," says Lowe, urging first timers to wait and see how much they enjoy the sport before committing themselves to a healthy investment.

Lowe sees nothing but success for a sport she feels has the brightest of futures. "Biathlons are up and coming," says Lowe. "They're the little brother of triathlons, but I think that with enough sponsorship we're going to see the biathlon come into its own. I really think it's going to be the next generation of multievent sport."

Lyle Parker
Alexandria, Louisiana
Age 31

Law school drove him to run, friendship drove him to bike, and swimming drove him to the biathlon, where Lyle Parker debuted in a big-time, small-town fashion—nipped by only 10 seconds at the Baton Rouge Medical Center Biathlon.

Parker, a native of Alexandria, Louisiana, has since gone on to bigger and better things. At the February 1988 Desert Princess World Championships, Parker placed a remarkable eighth in a field that included me, Mark Allen, Mike Pigg, Scott Tinley, Brad Kearns, and a host of other top professionals—this despite putting in a 40-hour week as a lawyer.

Parker came to the biathlon in a roundabout fashion. Attending law school in Baton Rouge, he picked up running to stave off the inevitable effects of too much desk time. Competitive by nature ("Anything I get into usually ends up being competitive in spirit"), Parker soon found himself logging 100-mile weeks. After graduating from law school, Parker landed a job in his hometown, where he became friends with cyclists who were members of a local bike club. He picked up cycling, a sport that didn't exactly grab him by the toe clips. "It took me a while to get interested," drawls Parker, "but I eventually did."

Parker had dabbled with swimming (as an injured runner he took to the pool), but swimming had always been his weak sport. More important, training for triathlons, says Parker, didn't leave him with much time. "Biathlons just seemed like something I could spend my time on and do well rather than spreading myself thin for triathlon," says Parker. "Picking up the biathlon was a matter of convenience."

Working as a lawyer can put a crimp in his training schedule, admits Parker, who compensates by training hard. Weekday bike rides and runs are squeezed in before and after work, and despite the drudgery, Parker spends a lot of time spinning away on a wind trainer. "I've become calloused to that experience," he laughs. Parker views weekends as a chance to pick up the slack; it's not uncommon for him to put in a two-and-a-half-hour run and 50-mile bike ride on Saturday, then follow that with a 90-mile ride and 10-mile run on Sunday. He is not, however, above taking a day off. "Don't hesitate to take a day off," advises Parker, who knows well the stress that a full work load and a full workout schedule can bring.

Parker's final advice to budding biathletes: do whatever you can to stay motivated, and do your best to establish a routine that makes working out a habit. This one-two punch, says Parker, will help you become the best biathlete you can be.

Russ Jones
Collingswood, New Jersey
Age 33

Russ Jones has had his share of bad luck in Bordentown, New Jersey. Two years in a row he found himself stranded at a truck stop just off the New Jersey turnpike. Year one found him standing by the interstate, short on time, bike over his shoulder, thumb pointed in the general direction of Staten Island. The next year offered a slight improvement; Jones was able to rely on the good graces of a friend. "They weren't planning on going to New York," beams Jones, "but somehow they squeezed me and my bike into their little two-door sedan."

Despite his broken-down car, Jones managed to arrive at the Staten Island Biathlon in time to win the race on both occasions.

If one thing can be said of Russ Jones, it's that little stands in his way. A mailman from Collingswood, New Jersey, Jones has managed to juggle a full-time job, family responsibilities (he is the father of two), New Jersey winters,

Photo courtesy of Russ Jones

Russ Jones.

and a less-than-dependable car to become one of biathlon's premier athletes.

Jones came to the biathlon with an enviable background. A runner in high school and college, Jones by age 24 had logged personal bests of 23:50 for five miles, 30:12 for 10K, 49:20 for 10 miles, and 2:18 for the marathon. Odds were he would remain a runner. But in 1983 his life changed when he was hit by a car. Two subsequent knee operations, a foot-long scar, and a right leg two inches shorter than the left slowed the competitive Jones enough to make him realize he would have to direct his efforts elsewhere if he wanted to remain competitive. He did and he has—winning biathlons up and down the East Coast.

Jones gave his first biathlon, "an oddball event somewhere in eastern Pennsylvania," little thought. However, in 1985 the New York Biathlon Series got underway and Jones got serious; since then he captured the overall series title each time. Although the New York series has served as his centerpiece, Jones estimates he has won some 25 biathlons since 1984.

His time limited by job and family, Jones has developed a minimalist's attitude toward training; workouts, squeezed in after work, are generally no longer than an hour to an hour and a half. Even if he had more time, his training wouldn't be much different. Jones's rationale is simple. Most biathlons are short, no longer than the popular 5K–30K–5K format. "Why do you have to go out and ride 50 miles a day when your longest ride is 25 miles?" asks Jones, whose longest ride is usually 20 miles.

There is, of course, a price to pay. Cutbacks in quantity necessitate increases in quality. Jones's workouts are hard and fast. On some days he will ride as little as eight miles, but he'll send his heart rate through the ceiling by riding 28 miles an hour. Weather permitting, Jones runs every day and rides four to five times a week. Since most biathletes come from a running background, Jones recommends a two-to-one ratio of biking to running; he generally runs 40–45 miles a week and bikes 80 miles a week. Jones's advice, sound and simple, is applicable to all recreational biathletes.

"Don't go overboard on mileage. You can get away with shorter runs and bikes than you think. Overtraining will simply make you more tired and more exhausted for the race."

Marc Bloom
Marlboro, New Jersey
Age 42

For 15 years, Marc Bloom was a committed member of the running boom. "I got tied in with the 'run every day, pile up the miles' marathon routine," says Bloom, who estimates that from 1972 until 1985 he ran an average of 50 miles a week, logged a half dozen marathons, and ran more than 100 other road races.

Bloom suffered through the usual assortment of running injuries, but it wasn't until three years ago, at age 39, that sciatica laid him low. A sports journalist and former editor of *The Runner* magazine, Bloom was well acquainted with the concept of total fitness. Advised by his doctor not to run, Bloom began dabbling in swimming and bicycling with mixed results. "The bicycling came easily, and it was also appealing," says Bloom. "The swimming I didn't take to that well."

Bloom competed in triathlons but found that three sports put too much of a dent in his time for home and work. Since he was not particularly enamored of swimming, turning to biathlons was not a difficult decision. Bloom entered his first biathlon in 1986; the following year he hit 16 races. "I guess I got hooked on bicycling the way I got hooked on running," he admits. He bought a $150 bicycle ("the cheapest thing I could find") and took to the roads.

Bloom, who writes a regular running column for the *New York Times*, is better acquainted, through both practice and theory, with the needs of runners turned cyclists. First, he says, don't expect miracles; just because you're a 2:30 marathoner doesn't mean you'll be an instant success as a cyclist. Second, prepare yourself for unaccustomed stress and strain; serious cycling isn't what you remember from your childhood days. Third, don't be shocked when your fitness doesn't suffer; cycling will force you to cut back on your running, says Bloom, but high-quality running mileage, coupled with the benefits of cycling, may make you leaner and meaner than you ever were. Finally, don't dive in head first; spend a few hundred dollars for an entry-level bike, then upgrade it after you're sure you like the sport. This may come sooner than you planned. Says Bloom: "I popped into a bike store for a pair of cleats and ended up with a $650 bike. Minus the cleats."

John Howard
Encinitas, California
Age 41

Captured by an ABC television camera from a helicopter 500 feet overhead, the vision of a smooth-flowing John Howard mowing down the field during the bike leg of the 1981 Hawaiian Ironman was a lesson in what efficient cycling can do. Howard came out of the swim seemingly out of the race. Five hours, 112 miles, and hordes of cyclists later he was in the lead for good.

Three-time Olympian in both the road race and the team time trial, seven-time national titlist, holder of the world speed record on a bike (152.2 mph), Howard saw the biathlon as a natural evolution. Swimming has always been his weak point, while cycling and running cater to his strengths. Though he is now more involved with coaching than competing, his brief forays into the biathlon have been successful—in 1986 he won his age group at the New York Biathlon Series National Championship in Central Park, placing fifth overall.

Though Howard's involvement with biathlons is limited, as a world-class cyclist his advice is invaluable. Though cycling is a complex sport with a thousand nuances, Howard boils it down to a few basics: "Get position, get comfortable, and spin." Proper position means making sure your bike is properly fitted, and, emphasizes Howard, it is crucial that an expert do this for you. Once properly positioned, stay comfortable on the bike and spin the pedals, keeping the gears low. Spinning in a low gear takes the strain off the knees, usually the first joint to go in a cyclist.

The easiest way to pick up these and the myriad other basics that will make you a better cyclist is to ride with an experienced group. Howard also recommends that biathletes mix speed with endurance in their training and bike and run hard on alternate days to avoid injury and burnout. Finally, advises Howard, pace yourself.

"Most people go out and just beat themselves up. I've seen this again and again," says Howard, who admits to being guilty of this himself. "Part of having a good time means pacing yourself. Try to have a good time; enjoy it. Don't get overly obsessed."

Bob Terry
Indianapolis, Indiana
Age 61

Bob Terry's evolution as a biathlete was more gradual than most. Ten years ago, Terry, 51 and suffering from a variety of health problems, was encouraged by his doctor to get out of the house and exercise. His doctor, a runner, recommended running, so Terry strapped on running shoes and walked out the door. As advised, he started slowly. "I'd walk a mile and run a block. Then I'd rest," he says.

Gradually, however, the walk-run format turned to a consistent jog. Then the jog became a run. "Then," says Terry, "I bought a bicycle."

At 55, Terry joined a local Indianapolis masters swimming program and rediscovered the joys of competitive swimming. He had swum competitively in high school and dabbled with swimming sporadically since, but the masters program gave him focus, provided competition, and piqued his curiosity. Could he do a triathlon?

The process was in full swing. In 1982 Terry did his first triathlon, a half-mile swim/ 12-mile bike/ four-mile run hosted by a local YMCA. "I finished it, and I felt really great," says Terry before adding the inevitable addendum. "It just whetted my appetite for more." Four years later, on a very hot day, he completed the Muncie (Indiana) Endura-thon, a 1.2-mile swim/56-mile bike/13-mile run.

Terry's first biathlon came in 1984 on the heels of a summer triathlon season. Local organizers were hosting the first annual Tuxedo Brothers Biathlon (see Index) and, says Terry, "It just seemed to fit. When I saw the entry form I just signed up right away."

Because of his swimming background, Terry focuses on the triathlon; biathlons fill the gaps at the beginning and the end of the season. From that first walk around the block he has worked himself up to a schedule that would make most people blanch: five days of swimming and running, three days of cycling and weight lifting. Cross-training, says Terry, lessens the strain on tendons and muscles, allow-ing him to exercise much more than single-sport athletes his age. And there are certain advantages that come with age. Terry smiles. "Younger guys that I know who are still working really envy my time."

And the older guys? Well, Terry admits to trying to cajole friends into triathlons and biathlons, but he says it's not for everyone. "You've got to enjoy it, and to do that you've got to have a little bit of competitive zeal," says Terry. If you do, that alone is enough. "I don't have to win, mind you; I don't even have to place," says Terry. "I just like to hear that gun go off."

Barbara Buchan
Leucadia, California
Age 32

For Barbara Buchan, the summer of 1982 doesn't exist; her last memory of that season is the sight of 20 cyclists going down in a heap. Buchan was the 21st and unluckiest—a fractured skull left her close to death.

Five brain surgeries, two reconstructed arms, and five years later, Barbara Buchan stood at the starting line of the Desert Princess Run-Bike-Run. Still a bit unsure of her

Photo courtesy of Barb Buchan

Barb Buchan.

abilities, she had enlisted the help of cyclist Charles Dempsey. Dempsey, who had lost his right leg in a car accident, would do the cycling leg, and Buchan would do the 5K runs on both ends. After the race was over, Dempsey confronted Buchan with the truth. "Charles said, 'I think you can do this whole thing, Barb,' " laughs Buchan. Two months later she did, completing the 5K–30K–5K course and finishing 12th in a field of 400. She was "really jazzed," says Buchan of a performance that also placed her fifth in her age group.

That performance was just one step in what has been a long, uphill climb. After her accident, Buchan gave more thought to recovering than competing. Yet thoughts of competing still flickered for the once national-caliber cyclist. Watching a 10K road race in San Diego three years after her accident, Buchan was approached by Ron Smith. Smith, a friend, asked Buchan how she was doing. "OK",

she replied, "but I sure would like to get back on a bike."
"Fine," said Smith. "Let's go."

Smith, a top masters triathlete, plopped Buchan back on a bike, and together they cautiously went through what had once been simple paces. "It was like beginning all over again," says Buchan. "I was so weak."

The initial goal was simple. Buchan's accident had left her with epileptic seizures. Since she was unable to drive, getting her back on a bike would at least give her freedom to get around town. But Buchan improved more quickly than Smith expected. Within six months she was racing against other disabled cyclists. Two years later, at the Desert Princess, she proved that she could run and bike with the able-bodied.

Now competing in cycling and track for the disabled, Buchan has found that her training has resulted in a very respectable biathlon. This does not mean, however, that she doesn't suffer like the rest of us. The memory of the second run at the Desert Princess biathlon is still a vivid memory.

"When I started, the quads were just like, ohhhhh, choke, choke, choke," laughs Buchan. "It's a definite challenge to get off the bike and run."

Tom Sullivan
Palos Verdes, California
Age 41

For Tom Sullivan, the biathlon truly has two facets. "For me the biathlon is the blending of individual achievement with people participation," says Sullivan. "Most people enter biathlons to be individual. I enter them as much to share as to be a competitor."

Blind from birth, Sullivan's name may ring a bell; his book *If You Could See What I Hear* has sold more than two million copies, and the movie of the same name has touched thousands of people.

Sullivan has been hip deep in sports ever since he started wrestling in the fourth grade. Never one to let blindness hold him back ("I was one of those kids who tried everything," says Sullivan, who once jumped off the roof of his high school to see how deep the snow really was), Sullivan wrestled his way to the 1968 Olympic Trials. "I think because of the blindness I had more need to win than the other kids did," he says.

Like most biathletes, Sullivan came to the sport from a triathlon background, and like many biathletes, Sullivan wasn't particularly enamored of the swim. Because he is blind, Sullivan competes with a partner. On the bike (tandem) and on the run, this poses little problem; Sullivan's partner simply has to have a knack for communicating clearly and quickly. The swim, however, presents a more difficult hurdle. "To know where you are is very difficult," says Sullivan. "The biathlon lends itself far better to me."

Sullivan, who ran track in high school, is no stranger to running. Cycling has never presented a problem either. As a boy growing up in New England he spent plenty of time on the family's Schwinn tandem. "No gears, the thing must have weighed 80 pounds," says Sullivan. Unfortunately, when Sullivan did his first biathlon in 1986, his equipment hadn't improved; a friend lent him a tandem that, though somewhat lighter, carried a few unneccessary extras. "It had a plastic flamingo mounted on the front fender," laughs Sullivan.

There was one other problem. Sullivan is six-feet, two-inches tall, usually much taller than his partners. The average tandem is designed to put the larger person in front—not a particularly sound idea if that person is blind. The end result? "It's like watching the Addams Family," says Sullivan. "The guy on the back is sort of like Lurch—he leans over the handlebars and breathes down the neck of the guy in the front." Centurion, however, is currently designing a customized, lightweight racing tandem that will eliminate Sullivan's vulturelike posture.

Sullivan's biggest limitation is not blindness but lack of time. A self-described actor, writer, producer, and singer,

Tom Sullivan (center) running the San Diego Marathon in 1987.

Sullivan has written four books, coproduced the television show "Fame," written musical scores, and become a hit on the campus and corporate lecture circuit. Add on regular appearances at the piano in places like Tahoe and Las Vegas and Sullivan spends some 300 days a year on the road. "It's hard for me to get the time to train well," says Sullivan, who spends a lot of time on stationary bikes and treadmills in health clubs across the country.

As a full-time professional and part-time athlete, Sullivan offers some sage advice to would-be biathletes. Before you pick up the sport, decide why you're in it. "Don't fool yourself," says Sullivan. "If you're going out there to have a wonderful experience, then that requires one kind of training. If you're going out there to be a competitor, then know that. If you say to yourself, 'I'm going to try hard,' but you're not fit, then you're probably going to be disappointed in your performance and the whole day won't make sense."

Mike ("Muddy") Waters
San Diego, California
Age 33

By now his coworkers are accustomed to Mike Waters's rapid comings and goings. "It's interesting," says Waters of his unconventional training regimen. "I run all day during work. I run from point A to point B. I hustle everywhere I go."

Thus Waters, a construction worker, lends new meaning to on-the-job training. His nine-to-five wind sprints, says Waters, serve as speed work. After work Waters logs a five-to-six-mile run and somewhere between 30 and 40 miles on

Mike ("Muddy") Waters
(right) and friend.

Photo courtesy of Mike Waters

the bike. Every day. "You know," says Waters, "I'm obsessed with this stuff."

Waters came to the biathlon on a whim. A traditional athlete at San Jose's Oak Grove High School, Waters played football, basketball, and baseball and was good enough to be nominated class athlete three years running. This, however, was as close as Waters ever came to running. Yet when a short triathlon cropped up in San Jose shortly after Waters graduated from college, he leaped at the opportunity. He had never swum or biked, and his running was limited to fast breaks and jogs to and from the dugout. No matter. Waters slogged his way through the swim, then picked his way through the crowd on the bike and the run. The love affair was immediate. "I thought, 'Wow, this is right up my alley.' "

There was, however, one problem. Waters suffers from what he calls the Joe Frazier disease, so dubbed because of the former heavyweight champion's less-than-efficient style in the water. "I saw him in a 'Superstars' competition," explains Waters, "and the other guys had finished the race before he was even halfway down the pool." Triathlons filled Waters's need for competition, but the swim was a bit of a headache. When a San Jose radio station hosted a bike-run, Waters entered and was hooked.

Intensely competitive, Waters once approached me at a race, told me how much he admired me, and in the next breath said he would eventually catch me. Though he has yet to beat me, Waters has narrowed the gap considerably, becoming a top contender in his age group. "My goal," he states flatly, "is to be the best in the world in my age group."

Susan Griesbach
Fullerton, California
Age 30

The run-bike format caters directly to the strengths of Susan Griesbach, one of biathlon's top performers. It also eliminates her only weakness: swimming. Griesbach still remembers her first triathlon.

"My arms were so tired I could hardly lift myself out of the pool at the end of the swim," says Griesbach. "It took me two tries to get out of the water."

Though her swimming has improved markedly (Griesbach has a series of consistently high finishes at some of triathlon's biggest races), Griesbach is first and foremost a cyclist. In September 1988 she set an American record for the 40K time trial. Griesbach has parlayed her cycling strengths into a first-class biathlon; if not for Liz Downing (see Index), she might be the sport's queen.

Griesbach came from a multisport background. "In high school I played basketball, volleyball, softball, and did track and field," says Griesbach. She also swam as a youngster but, she admits, not with a great deal of success. "I was a breast stroker, and I was pretty bad."

Ironically, Griesbach's track-and-field experience was

Susan Griesbach.

Photo courtesy of Susan Griesbach

mostly field—shot put and discus. She didn't take up running until 1980 when as a graduate student she picked up the sport "to help relieve stress and get in some kind of shape." Running also conformed to her typically irregular graduate-student schedule. "It was something you could do all hours of the day or night," she says.

Cycling followed four years later. In 1986 she registered with the USCF (United States Cycling Federation) and began racing with almost immediate success. From the beginning Griesbach displayed a gutsy and aggressive style—in her first year of competition she won the Western Section Category 4 road racing championship with a solo breakaway at the 12K mark of the 58K course.

All this has been accomplished while juggling a full-time job as a programmer-analyst for Chevron Oil. "I put a lot of time into it when I'm not at work," smiles Griesbach.

Though her schedule varies depending on what she is training for, Griesbach generally works out twice a day. Chevron provides its workers with a health club, and lunchtime, almost without fail, finds Griesbach spinning on a stationary bike or running around the track. During the biathlon season Griesbach runs at lunch, then cycles every evening, getting in long runs and rides on the weekends. She also swims four to five days a week; because she is still very involved in triathlons, it is something she simply cannot afford to ignore.

This sounds like the kind of schedule that would break the average mortal, and it may be. However, if you're training strictly for the biathlon, one of the sport's biggest advantages, says Griesbach, is time. Griesbach points out that most biathlons are shorter than triathlons and, without the swim, require less training.

"Biathlon fits in with more of a normal life," says Griesbach. "You don't have to be 150 percent devoted to training to do one. It's the kind of thing you can do and you haven't shot your whole weekend. You can still go home and go grocery shopping."

Photo by Al Zacharka/Kinematic Photography

Liz Downing, considered to be the best female biathlete in the world.

**Liz Downing
Portland, Oregon
Age 29**

Liz Downing began her athletic career as a runner at the ripe old age of nine, and by the time she reached college she was fed up with it. She spent her years at Portland's Lewis and Clark College playing basketball, softball, and soccer. But a lifetime of running is a hard thing to shake. Once out of college, Downing picked up running again, then began to ride her bike to work. Presto, biathlon's most formidable woman.

Like many biathletes, Downing came to the sport from the triathlon. Swimming was her weak point, and the biathlon catered to her blistering bike-and-run. She entered her first biathlon in July 1987, the National Championships in Ontario, California. She won, besting a field that included 1986 Ironman winner Paula Newby-Fraser and biathlon standout Susan Griesbach. "I guess I was a little surprised," says Downing, who entered the race because she happened to be in the area on business.

By the time Downing returned to Ontario in 1988 to defend her title, she had racked up six straight biathlon wins to become the sport's only undefeated woman. In Ontario she lengthened the streak to seven, winning the women's professional division by more than five minutes and finishing only eight minutes behind the men's winner—me.

Downing, who worked full-time until July 1987, currently puts in a 20-hour week for InSports, a Portland, Oregon, based running apparel manufacturer. She generally gets in two workouts a day, one a swim, the other a bike or run. Downing's workouts are also shorter than most of her competitors', stressing quality over quantity. There are, however, easy days. "You have to take time off," says Downing. "You just can't pound every day."

Because the bottom line, says Downing, is fun. Too often people dive right into the sport with serious intentions and expect to immediately establish themselves as a contender. It just won't happen, says Downing, who urges a more gradual approach.

"It just takes time; the longer you compete, the better you'll do. Have fun and success will come."

10
TRAINING CLUBS TO GET YOU GOING

Since biathlon is a relatively new sport, clubs expressly for biathletes are as rare as four-leaf clovers. Don't throw in the towel, however. If you're an aspiring biathlete looking for guidance and companionship (or someone to draft off of), your options are almost limitless; hundreds of running, cycling, and triathlon clubs across the country offer an ideal learning and training forum.

Finding these clubs is often as simple as walking through the door of your local bike shop or running-wear store. Though you may know these shops only as places that put a dent in your wallet, more often than not they also serve as information outlets. In fact, many bike shops and running-wear stores can provide you with more information than you could ever need—dozens of handouts and leaflets announcing everything from upcoming races to next Wednesday's training ride. These stacks of paper are usually displayed in some prominent place where you can help yourself.

If you can't find any of these loose-leaf libraries, just ask. The people who work in these stores are generally athletes themselves; even if they're not members of the local club, chances are they can point you in the right direction. Don't be shy. Most people like to talk about their interests, and athletes-cum-salespersons are no exception. Tell them you're a runner in search of cyclists and then sit back and let them bend your ear.

CYCLING CLUBS

It's a given that the majority of today's biathletes come from a running background. I did, and according to the United States Biathlon Federation so do 70 percent of my biathlete peers. If you fall into this category and are taking a serious look at the biathlon, it is crucial that you ride with other cyclists. Probably the best way to do this is through a bicycling club.

I won't pretend to be a cycling expert. I have learned a few things since I picked up the sport, but almost every single tip came from another cyclist. And I didn't learn these tidbits while sitting in a pizza parlor swilling beer; I learned them on the roads, hammering away with the pack. In cycling there is no substitute for experience, and nowhere will you find more experience than in a cycling club. If you ride alone you may satisfy your introspective urges, but you won't learn anything about gear selection, cadence, posture, or any of the seemingly endless nuances that will make you a better cyclist. Learning the ins and outs of a sport through hard knocks is all well and good, but there is no sense in suffering through easily avoidable pitfalls. Joining a cycling club allows you the luxury of picking the brains of those who have already made the mistakes.

This brings me to an important point. Cyclists have a reputation for being somewhat aloof, and there are more than a handful of stories (most of them true) of beginning cyclists who have gone on group rides only to be abused, spat on (literally), and then left to die (figuratively) by their more experienced counterparts. John Howard, a three-time Olympian who has now turned his cycling expertise to coaching, admits that "the elitists can be hard to reach" and says he has seen experienced cyclists completely ignore the presence (and questions) of beginners. Howard recommends you adopt a friendly and outgoing attitude and, as lemminglike as it may sound, blend in with the crowd. Cyclists, says Howard, are more apt to take you seriously if you look the part. This doesn't mean a $3,000 bicycle and a La Vie Claire (Greg Lemond's cycling team) jersey, but it does mean no cut-off jeans or football helmets. "If you look like a real nerd, you might get snubbed," admits Howard.

In defense of cyclists, some beginners bring this abuse on themselves. Charles Dempsey, a Category 2 cyclist (one step down from the pros) from Vista, California, says he has seen many beginners come to a group ride with a know-it-all attitude when it is quite obvious that they don't. Not only does not asking questions get you no answers, but it also quickly raises the ire of your fellow cyclists when you careen about in a pace line, posing a real danger to all. Come to the sport as the neophyte you are, and more than likely, says Dempsey, things will go smoothly.

"If you ask for help, most cyclists will help you," says Dempsey, "but if you're riding the pace line incorrectly, someone offers some constructive criticism, and you just tell them, 'Oh, I know what I'm doing, I've done this a million times,' then you may have problems. If you don't understand something or don't know how to do something, don't fake it. Ask someone."

By now you are probably planning on taking your chances solo. Don't. The word of warning was meant as just that. Most cyclists are more than willing to help. All that's required of you is an honest and friendly attitude, and most cyclists will respond in kind. If they don't, fine. It will make it all the more satisfying when you blow their doors off on that vicious uphill.

One final word about cycling with a group. Not only does it offer you a chance to pick up pointers, it also offers the ultimate conditioning tool. Granted, there are many biathletes who train on their own and some of them are quite successful, but I feel you get a far better workout by riding in a pack at 25 miles an hour than tottering head down into a head wind at eight miles an hour. For one thing, you can go much farther. High speeds in practice also accustom you to high speeds in races. And anyone who tells you that riding in a pack is easy obviously hasn't ridden in a pack. If you want scientific proof, use a heart monitor. I guarantee you that in a hard pace line your pulse will be going through the ceiling.

If you're still not quite sure about the cycling-club scene, find a group ride and test it out yourself. Most bike shops will have information about upcoming rides, which crop up throughout the week during the season. Most rides are rated, an efficient way of letting you know where you belong. If you're just beginning, don't get overzealous and pick a ride that's over your head. Pick a ride with a difficult rating, and you may find yourself riding up the biggest hill you've ever seen with nary a rider in sight. You have been, in cycling terms, punted, and odds are it will be a long and lonely ride home. Pick a ride and an ability level you can handle, and then work your way up from there.

RUNNING CLUBS

Up to this point I've concentrated on cycling clubs simply because, as I mentioned before, most biathletes are runners looking to learn cycling. Ironically, though, most biathletes involved in clubs probably belong to running clubs. Race director Joe Kratovil, who also serves as executive director for the U.S. Biathlon Federation, says biathlon clubs are already springing from running clubs. Thus, running clubs are probably the best place to turn. Many cyclists in cycling clubs view running as some sort of pagan ritual, but increasing numbers of runners are turning to cycling for variety and to ease wear and tear. Also, there are far more running clubs than cycling clubs; unless you live in the middle of the Mojave, chances are there's a running club in your area.

TRIATHLON CLUBS

Triathlon clubs also offer a good training and learning forum for the beginning biathlete. These clubs, especially the larger ones, usually have their fair share of competent and experienced athletes you can learn from. These trisport athletes can also offer valuable tidbits you might not find in running and cycling clubs, such as how to make quick transitions and how to shake the agony out of your legs when you come off the bike and go into the run. The only drawback to triathlon clubs is there aren't that many. The United States Triathlon Federation, the sport's governing body, listed some 130 clubs in 1988. This listing is by no means extensive, and unless you live in California or near a major city in the East, you'll probably stand a better chance of finding a running or cycling club.

Belonging to a club also offers a few other advantages. Dan Honig's New York–based Big Apple Triathlon Club, with some 1,500 members, sends out listings of races up and down the East Coast, publishes a newsletter called the *Tri-ing Times*, and puts on about a dozen races a year, offering discounts on entry fees to club members. Even the smaller clubs host races, and many bring in guest speakers, who will tell you everything you need to know from what to eat to how to make transitions. If the source is reliable, this kind of information can be invaluable. Membership fees are generally reasonable (a one-year membership with the Big Apple Triathlon Club is $20), and some clubs have no fees at all.

GOING SOLO

I should point out that most athletes—whether they be runners, cyclists, triathletes, or biathletes—generally go it alone. We've never been much of a club society, and this is reflected in the membership of cycling, running, and triathlon clubs. U.S. Biathlon Federation president Honig, once a former member of the U.S. Triathlon Federation, estimates that no more than 10 percent of all triathletes belong to a club, and that figure, says Honig, is probably a little high. Honig thinks this 10 percent figure also applies to running-club membership. Perhaps because of the nature of the sport, membership in cycling clubs is higher. Andy Bohlmann, director of technical services for the United States Cycling Federation (USCF), says 60–75 percent of the cyclists registered with the USCF belong to clubs.

There are sources to turn to if you're a biathlete without a club. The U.S. Biathlon Federation (P.O. Box 1596, Morristown, New Jersey 07961) offers a free, 12-week training schedule to prepare you for a typical 3 mile-20 mile-3 mile biathlon, along with a checklist of everything you'll need come race day. (Would you think of bringing extra safety pins for your race number?) You can usually find out about upcoming races by checking local bicycle and running stores or by picking up a copy of *Triathlete* magazine, which has begun listing biathlons in its triathlon calendar.

Whether you belong to a recognized club isn't important—but I do think it's important to train with others. This is especially true if you're just getting started and don't know a toe clip from a transition. But to be honest, I think it's equally important no matter how far you've progressed. Training alone can be a grind; it's a lot easier to face a 60-mile training ride when you know you'll be suffering with others. You may also be more apt to show up—even on days when I don't really feel like training, I'd rather face the blahs than the jeers of my training partners when I don't materialize. And when I do show up even though I'm not really in the mood, group rides and runs drive me to push myself far harder than if I were alone and feeling sorry for myself. There's nothing like a few breakaways to get your mind back into training.

Appendix

There are hundreds of clubs around the country where you can find someone to run or ride with. Here are a few to get you started.

Anchorage Youth Tri-Club
Contact: Michael Crane
8160 Northview Drive
Anchorage, Alaska 99504

Viaduct Vultures
Contact: Job Montgomery
3499 Independence Drive
Birmingham, Alabama 35213

Greater Arizona Bike
Association
PO Box 43273
Tucson, Arizona 85733

Southern Arizona Road Runners
PO Box 40728
Tucson, Arizona 85717

Triple Sweat LA
Contact: Dan Gardner
265 South Robertson Boulevard
#6249
Los Angeles, California 90211

Orange County Tri Club
Contact: Dorothy Miller
622 Hamilton #7
Costa Mesa, California 92627

Fresno Area Racing and
Training
Contact: Earl Taylor
5588 North Palm
Fresno, California 93704

Santa Monica Triathlon Club
Contact: Heather Clare
31697 Sea Level Drive
Malibu, California 90265

Triathletics West
Contact: Mark Evans
PO Box 8040-128
Walnut Creek, California 94596

Tri Valley Triathletics
Contact: Paula Harris
4209 Abbington Court
Westlake Village, California
92361

Cabrillo Cycling Club
Contact: Walt Spieth
1636 Hornblend
San Diego, California 92117

Triathlon Club of Colorado
PO Box 6325
Denver, Colorado 80206

First State Triathlon Club
Contact: Dan Rich
24 Brandywine Boulevard
Wilmington, Delaware 19809

Panama City Triathletes and
Biathletes
7125 North Lagoon Drive
Panama City Beach, Florida
32407

Miami Runners Club
Contact: Michael Peyton
14625 SW 64th Avenue
Miami, Florida 33156

Dayton Endurance Athletes
778 Jimmy Ann Drive #1610
Daytona Beach, Florida 32018

Atlanta Tri-Train Club
1601 Bretwood Drive
Ulburn, Georgia 30247

Big Island Tri and Bi Club
Contact: J. Curtis Tyler III
PO Box N
Kailua Kona, Hawaii 96745

Downtown Sports Club
441 North Wabash
Chicago, Illinois 60611

North Shore Athletics
PO Box 1751
Covington, Louisiana 70434

Race Pace Tri-Shop
6600 C. Baltimore
Baltimore, Maryland 21228

Sports Club
Department 2375
Hubbard University
Ann Arbor, Michigan 48109

Upper Midwest Triathlon
Association
PO Box 16303
Minneapolis, Minnesota 55416

The Midlands
2917 South 134th Avenue
Omaha, Nebraska 68144

Triathlon Club of New Mexico
14 Walter SE
Albuquerque, New Mexico 87102

Big Apple Biathlon Association
Contact: Dan Honig
301 East 79th Street #30
New York, New York 10021

Club Red Line
700 Columbus Avenue
New York, New York 10025

Farmington Athletic Club
PO Box 91-150
Wells Street West
Farmington, Ohio 44491

Solo Sports
8348 Wicklow Avenue
Cincinnati, Ohio 45236

Tulsa Wheelmen
PO Box 52242
Tulsa, Oklahoma 74152

Philadelphia Tri-Sport Club
3767 Lankenau Road
Philadelphia, Pennsylvania
19131

Spartansburg YMCA Striders
280 South Pine Street
Spartansburg, South Carolina
29302

Music City Tri/Bi Club
524 American Drive
Nashville, Tennessee 37211

Permian Basin Road Runners
PO Box 10483
Midland, Texas 79702

Cycle, Surf, and Turf
4322 North Haven Road
Dallas, Texas 75229

The Sporting Club
8250 Greensboro Drive
McLean, Virginia 22102

Skyline Racquet and Health
Club
5715 Leesburg Pike
Bailey's Cross Roads, Virginia
22041

Badger Tri Club
PO Box 1452
Milwaukee, Wisconsin 53224

For more information on where to find a cycling, running, or triathlon club in your area, contact:

Running: The Athletics Congress (TAC)
            200 South Capital Street
            Suite 140
            Indianapolis, Indiana 46225

Cycling: United States Cycling Federation (USCF)
            1750 East Boulder Street
            Colorado Springs, Colorado 80909

Triathlon: Tri Fed U.S.A.
            PO Box 1010
            Colorado Springs, Colorado 80901-1010

Biathlon: Big Apple Biathlon Club
            Cherokee Station
            PO Box 20427
            New York, New York 10028-9991

INDEX

Abdominal pain, 137
Abdominal strength, building,
  80–84
Abdominal stretch, 57
Aerodynamic handlebars, 17,
  18–19
AERO handlebars, 18–19
Aerohead helmet, 13
Allen, Mark, xiii, 7, 10, 28,
  110, 112–13, 119, 142, 143,
  144, 162
Anaerobic threshold (A.T.), 89,
  91
Anchorage Youth Tri-Club, 187
Ankle pain, 136
Anterior pelvic tilt, 80
Athletics Congress (TAC), 189
Atlanta Tri-Train Club, 188
Avia, 22

Badger Tri Club, 189
Baker, Liz, 47
Ballistic stretching, 62

Barrios, Arturo, 49, 90
Berenda, Sue, 50
Berglund, Marianne, 127
Biathlete
  clothing for, 126
  determining maximal heart
    rate, 93–95
  selecting performance level,
    93
  training tips for hard-core,
    89–91
Biathlon
  competitors in, 2–4
  finding clubs on, 189
  future for, 10
  growth of, 4–5
  history of, 1–2
  and locality, 5–10
  strengthening for, 153–54
Biathlon events, 139–41
  Bi-Icycle (Saskatchewan,
    Canada), 152

Coors Light Biathlon Series, xiii, 1, 5, 63, 108, 111, 113, 118, 144–46, 160

Desert Princess run-bike-run (Palm Springs, CA.), 9, 10, 26, 140, 141–42, 160, 169

New York Biathlon Series, 143–44

Ontario (California) Biathlon, 149–50

Princeton (New Jersey) Forrestal Village Biathlon, 146–48

Texas Cyruthon Series, 148–49

Tuxedo Brothers Biathlon (Indianapolis, Indiana), 151, 169

West Coast Biathlon Series (Venice Beach, CA.), 150–51

Biathlon survival kit
for cycling, 87
for running, 87

Biathlon trouble shooter's guide, 135–38
abdominal pain, 137
ankle pain, 136
heel pain, 136
knee pain, 136
low-back pain, 137
neck and shoulder pain, 137–38
thigh pain, 136
toe pain, 135
wrist and hand pain, 138

Bicycle, 82. *See also* Cycling
buying right, 12–19
cost of, 12–13
deciding where to buy, 14
fitting, to rider, 14, 16–18
test ride of, 14
training on the, 63–65

Bicycle shoe, 22

Bicycle Warehouse, 160

Bicycling helmets, 13

Big Apple Biathlon Association, 188

Big Apple Biathlon Club, 1, 189

Big Apple Triathlon Club, 185

Big Island Tri and Bi Club, 188

Bi-Icycle (Saskatchewan, Canada), 152

Bloom, Marc, 166–67

Body surfing, 133

Bohlmann, Andy, 186

Boogie boarding, 133–34

Briggs, L. J., 148

Brooklyn Biathlon, 1

Buchan, Barbara, 169–71

Bud Light USTS National Triathlon Championships, 119

Cabrillo Cycling Club, 188

Carr, Don, 151

Chek, Paul, 30–32, 52–62, 80–84, 102–4, 122–26, 135–38, 153–54

Circuit training, 153

Clark, Brenda, 7–8, 142

Clipless pedal, 16

Clip-on pedals, 18

Club Red Line, 188

Coors Light Biathlon, 01, 1, 5, 10, 63, 108, 111, 113, 118, 144–46, 160

Cross-country skiing, 129

Cross crunch, 87

Cross-training, 169

Crunch, 81–83

Cruz, Joaquim, 121

Curative massage, 124–25

Cycle, Surf, and Turf, 189

Cycling, 4, 11-12, 87. *See also* Bicycle
  biathlon survival kit for, 87
  buying the right bike, 12-19
  developing power, 27-28
  developing technique, 19-26
  finding clubs on, 189
  group riding, 11-12, 24, 28-29, 183-84
  and indoor turbo training workout, 33-43
  for speed, 26-27
Cycling accessories, cost of, 18
Cycling clubs, 182-84
Cycling pack, 76

Dayton Endurance Athletes, 188
Dempsey, Charles, 170, 183
Desert Princess Biathlon, 9, 10, 26, 140, 141-42, 160, 169
Desoto, Emilio, 21
Devlin, Jeff, 10, 113, 117, 119, 147
Dixon, Rod, 98
Downing, Liz, 143, 146, 176, 178-79
Downtown Sports Club, 188
Draft, 25

Effleurage, 31

Farmington Athletic Club, 188
Fat-Tire Biathlon Series, 6
First State Triathlon Club, 188
5K race or time trial, 94
Five-to-eight-minute test, 94
Foot strike, 52
Frazier, Joe, disease, 175
Fresno Area Racing and Training, 187
Fulton, Bill, 9

Gallo, Don, 152
Gears, 24
Glutes stretch, 59
Goal establishment, 97
  base, 97-99
  speed, 99-100
  strength, 99j
Greater Arizona Bike Association, 187
Great Swamp Biathlon, 146, 147
Griesbach, Susan, 175-77, 178
Grip shifts, 18
Groin and hamstring stretch, 58
Groin stretch, 59
Group bicycle riding, 11-12, 24, 28-29, 183-84

Hamstring stretch, 56
Handlebars, 17
Hanssen, Kirsten, 130
Heart rate, 89, 91
Heart-rate ranges
  base range, 96
  maximal range, 95
  threshold range, 95-96
Heel pain, 136
Hegg, Steve, 12
Heiden, Eric, 130
Hill climbing, 22-23
Hill running, 99
Hoffman, Norm, 93
Hogan, Rob, 149-50
Honig, Dan, 1, 2, 5-6, 10, 143-44, 185, 186
Hooker, Gary, 89, 93
Howard, John, 15, 25, 27, 167-68, 182-83

Ice skating, 130
If You Could See What I Hear (Sullivan), 171

Indoor turbo training workout,
    33–43
    ladder work, 37–38
    race-course simulation, 39
Injuries, 102–4
In-line skating, 130
Ironman, 01
Isom, George, 148–49

Joe Frazier disease, 175
Jones, Russ, 163–65
Joyce, Monica, 47

Kauai Triathlon, 9
Kayaking, 131
Kearns, Brad, 8, 9, 110, 142,
    162
Klein, Greg, 9, 142
Klem, Greg, 7–8
Knee pain, 136
Kratovil, Joe, 6, 139, 140,
    146–48, 184

Larson, Jay, 119
Latissimus dorsi and quadratus
    lumarum stretch, 60
Leach, Bill, 17
Lemond, Greg, 183
Line, learning to hold, 23–24
Locality, and biathlons, 5–10
Locke, Steve, 151
Low-back pain, 137
Lowe, Laura, 160–61

MacNaughton, Andrew, 110
Macy, Bob, 33
Max h.r., 93
McCartney, Kathleen, 109
Megamileage, 01
Miami Runners Club, 188
Microtrauma, 59
Midlands, 188
Milford-Holland Biathlon, 156
Mitchell, Bruce, 150–51

Molina, Scott, xiii, 2, 8, 9, 28,
    71, 142
Moonlight Bikes, 16
Mountain biking, 128–29
Mountain Man Triathlon, 129,
    130
Muscle tear, 59
Music City Tri/Bi Club, 189

National Biathlon
    Championship, 143
Neck and shoulder pain,
    137–38
Newby-Fraser, Paula, 148, 178
New York Biathlon Series,
    143–44
Nice, Mike, xiii
Noel, Anna, 145–46
North Shore Athletics, 188

Ocean sports, 131
Ontario (California) Biathlon,
    149–50
Orange County Tri Club, 187
Overtraining, 107

Panama City Triathletes and
    Biathletes, 188
Pape, Bill, 158–59
Parker, Lyle, 162–63
Pedaling, technique of, 19
Peloton, 76
Permian Basin Road Runners,
    189
Petrissage, 31–32
Philadelphia Tri-Sport Club,
    188
Pierce, George, 9–10
Pigg, Mike, xiii, 10, 67, 110,
    119, 142, 144, 162
Postevent massage, 124
Posture, proper, for running,
    51

Power, developing, 27–28
Pre-event massage, 122–23
Princeton (New Jersey)
    Forrestal Village Biathlon,
      10, 139, 146–48
Prolight bicycling helmet, 13
Pull, 76

Quadriceps stretch, 60, 61

Race, 105, 113
  day of, 110–17
  first run, 113
  four weeks before, 105–6
  night before, 109–10
  preparing equipment for,
    108–9
  ride in, 115–16
  second 5K, 117–20
  second transition, 116–17
  three weeks before, 106
  transition, 114–15
  two weeks before, 106
  week before, 106–7
  Race day, 110–17
  getting warmed up, 113
  setting up transition area,
    111–12
Race Pace Tri-Shop, 188
Recovery time, 124
Rectus femoris stretch, 58
Ride, 115–16
Rider, Walt, 110
Ripple, Jan, 148
Robinson, Harold, 144
Rock, Dan, 16, 18, 33, 74, 117
Rollerblades, 130
Rosarito-Ensenada Fun Ride,
    24
Running, 41
  biathlon survival kit for, 87
  finding clubs on, 189
  selecting proper shoes for,
    41–50

Running clubs, 184
Running technique, 51
  advanced drills for, 54
  and foot strike, 52
  proper posture, 51
  and skipping drill, 52–54

Santa Monica Triathlon Club,
    187
Santas, Kathy, 156–57
Santas, Mark, 156–57
Schuster, Richard, 42–48, 50
Schwarzenegger, Arnold, 11
Scott, Steve, 121
Scott handlebars, 18–19
Self-massage, 30–32
Sheehan, George, 41
Shoes, selection of, for
    running, 41–50
Skipping drill, 52–54
Skyline Racquet and Health
    Club, 189
Smith, Ron, 127, 170–71
Snowshoeing, 129–30
Solo riding, 185–86
Solo Sports, 188
Southern Arizona Road
    Runners, 187
Souza, Ken, 85–86, 122
Spangler, Dave, 93
Spartansburg YMCA Striders,
    188
Speed, 99, 101
  cycling for, 26–27
Speed skating, 130
Speed workouts, 101
Spin-Coach attachment, 33
Sporting Club, 189
Sports Club, 188
Sports massage, 122–26
  curative massage, 124–25
  postevent massage, 124
  pre-event massage, 122–23
  training massage, 123

Staten Island Biathlon, 163
Stewart, Greg, 118, 142
Straight-leg crunch, 81
Strength, 99
Strengthening, for biathlon,
    153–54
Stretching, 52–62
    reasons for, 56–58
    technique in, 60–62
Stretch reflex, 61, 62
Sub-max test, 96–97
Sullivan, Tom, 171–74
Sunglasses, 14
Surfing, 131, 133
Surf skiing, 131
Swimming, 130–31, 139

TAC (Athletics Congress), 189
Tandem riding, 20
10K or 10-mile time trials, 95
Terry, Bob, 168–69
Texas Cyruthon Series, 148–49
Thigh pain, 136
Thompson, Joel, 9, 10, 67, 110,
    117, 120, 141, 145
Tinley, Scott, xiii, 10, 28, 44,
    110, 112, 142, 162
Toe pain, 135
Training clubs, 181–82
    cycling clubs, 182–84
    running clubs, 184
    solo riding, 185–86
    triathlon clubs, 185
Training massage, 123
Training program
    bicycle, 63–65
        cornering, 65
        hill riding, 66
        importance of quality, 67
        maintaining line, 65–66
        momentum, 65
        power trips, 66
        specific training program,
            67–79

body surfing, 133
boogie boarding, 133–34
building abdominal strength,
    80–84
cross-country skiing, 129
establishing goal in, 97–101
ice skating, 130
in-line skating, 130
mountain biking, 128–29
snowshoeing, 129–30
speed skating, 130
surfing, 131, 133
swimming, 130–31
weight training, 127–28
year-long program for, 85–86
Training tips, for biathlete,
    89–91
Transition, 114–15
    second, 116–17
Transition area, setting up
    your, 111–12
Triathlete magazine, 186
Triathletics West, 187
Triathlon, xii
    finding clubs on, 189
    growth of, 1
Triathlon Club of Colorado,
    188
Triathlon Club of New Mexico,
    188
Triathlon clubs, 185
Tri Fed U.S.A., 189
Triple Sweat LA, 187
Tri Valley Triathletics, 187
Tug's Tavern swim-run-swim,
    2
Tulsa Wheelmen, 188
Turbo trainer, 33
    riding on, 19–20
Tuxedo Brothers Biathlon, 151,
    169

U.S. Biathlon Federation, 143,
    186
U.S. Cycling Federation
    (USCF), 186, 189
Upper Midwest Triathlon
    Association, 188

Van Arsdale, Ted, 52–53, 54
Vertical bounce, 54
Viaduct Vultures, 187
Visualization, 49
VO$_2$-max, 89, 91, 93–94
Vortechs Pedal, 16

Warren, Tom, 2
Waters, Mike (Muddy), 174–75
Weight training, 127–28
Weight-training machines, 153
West Coast Biathlon Series
    (Venice Beach, CA.),
    150–51
Wrist and hand pain, 138

Zuilhof, John, 148